WHEN A POPE ASKS
FORGIVENESS

WHEN A POPE ASKS
FORGIVENESS

The Mea Culpa's of John Paul II

Luigi Accattoli

Translated by
Jordan Aumann, OP

ALBA·HOUSE   NEW·YORK

SOCIETY OF ST. PAUL, 2187 VICTORY BLVD., STATEN ISLAND, NEW YORK 10314

ST PAULS

Originally published in Italian by Arnaldo Mondadori Editore,
S.p.A., Milan under the title *Quando il Papa chiede perdono.*

Library of Congress Cataloging-in-Publication Data

Accattoli, Luigi.
    [Quando il Papa chiede perdono. English]
    When a Pope asks forgiveness : the mea culpa's of Pope John
Paul II / Luigi Accattoli ; translated by Jordan Aumann.
        p.   cm.
    Includes bibliographical references.
    1. John Paul II, Pope, 1920-   —Quotations. 2. Catholic Church—
History—Quotations, maxims, etc. 3. Christianity and justice—Catholic
Church—Quotations, maxims, etc. I. Title.
BX1378.5.A3213   1998
230'.2.—dc21   97-45147
                                                            CIP

Table of Contents

PART ONE
Historical and Ecumenical Precedents

PART TWO

Pronouncements by John Paul II

Editor's Note

There are two concepts which recur frequently in the following pages that might be either ambiguous or misleading to the reader. The first has to do with the phrase "revision of history." In the context it has nothing to do with writing a "revisionist" version of history which would exculpate the Church from past wrongdoings or deny unsavory facts that occurred in the course of that history. Quite the contrary. It is the Pope's desire to re-examine the facts of history in the light of the truth and to take full responsibility for both the good and the bad so that the Church can move forward into the next millennium free from the burden of protecting its "image." The second has to do with the term "integralism." It refers to a tendency and a movement that arose in the Catholic Church about the time of Pope Pius X's condemnation of Modernism in 1907 and which resulted in the rise of an organization (the Sodalitium) that almost fanatically carried out his recommendations for vigilance against doctrinal deviations. The Sodalitium was suppressed by Pope Benedict XV who declared that in matters that the Church has left open to discussion moderation should reign and not unbased suspicions about the orthodoxy of opponents. The "integralist" mentality still exists in some quarters today, and is one of the things that Pope John Paul II addresses in his mea culpa's.

Preface:
An Examination of Conscience

This book contains a collection of ninety-four quotations in which Pope John Paul II admits the past faults of the Church or asks pardon for them. And these are certainly not all. In twenty-five of these excerpts, the Pope uses the expression "I ask forgiveness" or its equivalent.

These texts are the most interesting of his entire pontificate, and his words are open wide to the future. They are surely very personal, for no one can put in the mouth of the Pope any expression of repentance for the Crusades or the religious wars. And no one can pit one pope against another pope.

Sometimes the Pope's statements have aroused public interest and have ended up on the front pages of the newspapers or on the news broadcasts of radio and television. But more often they have passed unnoticed. Few of the persons who discuss these matters are capable of making an objective critical evaluation, but that is precisely what we intend to do in this book, which is at once an anthology and a bibliography of readings.

We believe that this is the first time that these quotations have been collected and published. We also believe that the "examination of conscience at the end of the millennium," proposed by Pope John Paul II, is the mature fruit of his pontificate and his most dynamic heritage. It is of great cultural interest as well and, for that reason, ought to be well received by those outside the Church.

Very likely the results of this "examination of conscience" will enter into tomorrow's textbooks. An investigation of the Eastern Schism, the case of Galileo, the Crusades, the Inquisition, the religious wars, etc., will reveal that one of the protagonists has at last changed its position or ideas. In these closing days of the second millennium, the Roman Pontificate is the only entity that speaks the same language that it spoke at the beginning and continues to accept responsibility for all its past.

How did Pope John Paul II arrive at this proposal of an examination of conscience at the end of the millennium? In the beginning there were sporadic admissions of responsibility for particular events and occasional requests for pardon, but the accumulation of facts and the reciprocal discovery of other incidents led to the second phase, namely, a self-examination at the end of the millennium. We shall follow a similar procedure, passing from particular pronouncements to the all-inclusive summations. In the beginning, as we have said, there were statements on a variety of topics. Here we shall mention a few that are especially relevant.

For example, during his visit to the Czech Republic in May of 1995, the Pope referred to the religious wars and then said: "Today, in the name of all Catholics and as Pope of the Church of Rome, I ask forgiveness for the

Y2K & YOU!

"IF Jesus Comes Back, Will I Be Left Behind?"

Today many people are concerned about the coming of the New Millennium. They fear that the end is near and that Christ may soon return. Are such concerns and fears justified? What should be the Christian's response to the Y2K? What does the Bible really say about the rapture, the coming of Christ, and the end of the world? The Sunset Church of Christ invites you to join us in a discussion of *Y2K AND YOU!*

"IF Jesus comes back, will I be left behind?"

Sunset Church of Christ
34ᵗʰ & Memphis
Lubbock, TX 79410

Sundays at 9:00 a.m.

fears about the arrangement, especially since she and Ben had already raised two sons and daughters of their own and have five grandchildren. Eventually, though, she said love conquered all the doubts.

"Love is a very strong emotion," she said. "We loved the children so much and we couldn't let them go. How could we sleep at night without knowing what they're doing?"

The adoption was final in April, and the couple has not fostered since then in order to give more attention to the new family members. They plan to bring in more foster children in a few months.

According to Frances, fostering children in the home was something she desired as a teenager.

"My sister and I would talk

whom were school age by their own request.

"We wanted school-age children so I could help them with school and with setting goals and help them learn the value of education," she said. "We didn't care about race. We wanted all the children to know that there is love in the world — that there are adults who will care for them."

The Hernandez home, which Ben renovated to twice its size to accommodate their growing family, still bears witness to those who have passed through its halls. A smattering of portraits scattered in the den and along the fireplace mantel are reminders of the young lives — both biological and otherwise — who have called the house home.

According to Susan Moeller, a foster/adoption recruiter with the Texas Department of Protective and Regulatory Services, injustices inflicted on non-Catholics in the course of the troubled history of these peoples."

In his Encyclical, *Ut Unum Sint* (May, 1995), after acknowledging that most other Christians suffer painful memories, he said: "To the extent that we are responsible for these, I join my predecessor Paul VI in asking forgiveness."

Again, in the month of May, 1995, in his message marking the fiftieth anniversary of World War II, the Pope stated that "the Christians of Europe need to ask forgiveness, even while recognizing that there were varying degrees of responsibility in the events which led to the war."

On yet another occasion, in his message to the indigenous peoples of the Americas (October 21, 1992), he said: "As Pastor of the Church, I ask you in the name of Jesus Christ to pardon those who have offended you; I ask you to pardon those who have caused pain to you and your ancestors during these 500 years."

In our research it is to this voice that we want to give all our attention. It speaks of the "injustices" of the Church in the confrontation between faith and science; the "temptation of an intransigent integralism" which characterized medieval Christianity; the responsibility of the men in the Church for discrimination against women; the forced conversions that accompanied the ruthless conquest of continents and peoples; the "errors" of anti-Semitism and the axiom, *cuius regio eius religio* (the people of a territory must follow the religion of their ruler).

Obviously, these individual instances of the mea culpa's are not what is meant by an examination of conscience at the end of the millennium; and even when viewed collectively, they do not qualify as such. The examination is the final stage which Pope John Paul II reaches after many years; it is the culmination of an inquiry which, in turn, prompts yet another investigation. Here also it is necessary to begin with his words, listening to what he has said and how he first formulated his proposal.

On one occasion the Holy Father said to the journalist, Jas Gawronski: "At the end of this second millennium we must make an examination of conscience: where we are, where Christ has brought us, where we have deviated from the Gospel."

Where have we deviated? It was from this question that the proposal for an examination of conscience was born. The question itself is indicative of the dramatic and multi-faceted personality of Pope John Paul II. His apostolic zeal does not leave him in peace, nor can he leave the Church and the world in peace. The question shows that he is the most restless of all believers and, perhaps, of all non-believers in this age.

The particular acknowledgment of a fault could have been prompted by some chance circumstance, such as an encounter with the descendants of persons who have suffered injustice. Thus, a meeting with native Indians may prompt one to investigate the Church's treatment of generations of Indians. But the examination of conscience at the end of the millennium is a general examen rather than a particular one; it is a response to a general, all-embracing sense of guilt rather than a specific fault. Then the question arises: where have we deviated from the Gospel? Pope John Paul asks this question, prompted by a sense of failure, a sense of responsibility which re-opens in Catholicism a heated discussion which had been discontinued after the Second Vatican Council.

But with so many supporters, why are so many opposed to the mea culpa's of Pope John Paul II? The historical and geographical cohesion of the Catholic Church is the reason for its power and influence, but it is also the reason for its sluggishness. Pope John Paul would like to preserve the cohesion of the Church and at the same time accelerate its activity. With the instinct of an apostle, he senses that the mission of the Church to the nations *(ad gentes)* calls for a revision of the historical image of the Church.

He has promoted this revision, and he does so without being intimidated by the opposition he encounters or by the statues and tombs of his predecessors. They call for respect for the past, but he does not hesitate to challenge the past with the zeal of an apostle.

For an ancient institution such as the Catholic Church, nothing is more difficult than to "revise" its history; that is to say, its image. Nevertheless, the Pope is convinced that this re-examination is necessary for the proclamation of the Gospel to the men and women of the second millennium; but even prior to that, it is demanded out of a sense of loyalty and truth in confronting oneself, one's own experience, one's own conscience.

Pope John Paul is aware of the acceleration of history during his lifetime and he realizes that the revolutionary changes of the Second Vatican Council have been too rapid for the general body of the Church to absorb. He seems to feel that the continuing updating of the memory of history, confided to the theological faculties and the Congregation for the Causes of Saints, is taking too much time, in view of the acceleration symbolically represented by the passage into a new millennium.

Prompted by the Second Vatican Council and the example of Pope John XXIII and Pope Paul VI, the Holy Father has chosen the end of the second millennium for an epochal mea culpa which will free his Church in part from "the burden of the dead" and prevent it from remaining a prisoner of its past. Two new elements have been added to the work of the re-examination of history that was introduced by the Second Vatican Council and the popes who reigned during its years:

— the first, which has been operative since the beginning of this pontificate, is the ever-increasing acknowledgment of responsibility for the accumulation of injustices committed by Catholic entities in various fields of activity throughout the centuries, which today the Catholic Church considers indefensible and unacceptable;

— the second, which was proposed in the spring of 1994 with a view to the Jubilee Year, is that the entire Catholic community should make an examination of conscience at the end of the second millennium in order to admit the serious cases of counterwitness by the "sons of the Church" during the last five centuries, and especially by anti-Semitism and in the courts of the Inquisition.

Our study is divided into two parts. The first part gives the historical setting for the mea culpa's and the examination of conscience; that is, the historical and ecumenical antecedents; the path that Pope John Paul II has traversed and anything new that he has introduced; the opposition he has encountered; and possible future developments. The second part is a detailed report and commentary on ninety-four quotations, divided into twenty-one chapters and extending from the Crusades to the treatment of Blacks. In all these instances, the Pope has corrected an opinion, admitted a fault, expressed regret, or asked for forgiveness.

When I started the actual research, after completing the chronicle of the papal pronouncements, I had no idea of the extent of the material, the coherence and consistency of Pope John Paul's thought, its development through the years, and the originality of the language and gestures that accompanied it.

With this project the Pope completes the work of the Second Vatican Council and makes his Church take a step forward, possibly a definitive step for its full insertion into the ecumenical movement. But it also introduces a new apologetics by modifying the image of the papacy and adjusting the role of the Catholic Church in the contemporary cultural panorama.

I have said that he completes the work of the Council, because by highlighting the areas of darkness in the millennium that is now ending, the Pope leads—as he wants to lead—to the light of the Gospel and the teachings of the Second Vatican Council. This rereading of history which, as we shall see, was previously sketched out by the Council, is what Pope John Paul wants to bring to completion. Of course, it is risky to give the Second Vatican Council a retroactive power. It calls for a great deal of prudence; but no one can say that up to this time the Pope has been imprudent in admitting the injustices of the past.

There are two elements in the next development in the ecumenical movement:

— "the purification of the historical memory," facilitated by each mea culpa, will foster an encounter between ancient adversaries;

— the adoption of a method of "confession of sin" as used in the churches of the Reformation. The "confession of sins" has never been neglected in the liturgy, but this places Catholicism in the school of their separated brethren concerning a matter that is not of secondary importance.

This is also a question of apologetics, which is a defense of the faith of the Church. With the examination of conscience at the end of the millennium, Pope John Paul II will overcome, or perhaps overturn, the controversial tone of Catholic apologetics and put in its place a historically unedited version that is more in keeping with the culture of freedom and tolerance. In this enterprise of his pontificate, which is its most mature fruit, Pope John Paul is saying that the world has deviated, but the Church has also deviated. Only by admitting this can the deviation be corrected.

But not everyone, even among the cardinals, shares the Pope's missionary zeal and his eagerness to achieve unity. Many persons feel that by admitting the deviations of Christians, the continuity and historical identity of the Catholic Church, which is perhaps the institution that is most ancient and most true to itself in the world today, is being compromised. From this come the words of warning from the Consistory. They all sound very reasonable, but they come from persons who do not share the apostolic zeal of Pope John Paul. And yet, no one in the Catholic Church has raised his voice to silence the Pope; so, after listening to the objections, he again expresses his intention.

No one can silence the Pope, and only the Pope can really say mea culpa for the Catholic Church. To bring up its own past against the Church, or simply to confront the Church with its past, could be equivalent to opposing popes of the past; and only a pope can contradict another pope. Neither Roncalli nor Montini dared to say as cardinals how much their ideas had matured and developed; and even Wojtyla was able to express fully his own maturity as a member of the Second Vatican Council and as a Pole only after he was elected Pope.

I believe that if he lives long enough, Pope John Paul will go ahead with his intention that the Church should follow him in this examination of conscience, or else he will do it alone, or practically alone. Looking at the Consistory, he can see that one moves more quickly alone; and the Pope is in a hurry. The year 2000 is approaching, and if the Pope is still with us in 2000, he will be eighty years old.

Up to the present time, except for the examination of the Galileo case, in which Pope John Paul had the help of a pontifical commission, and the implementation of a judicial inquiry of anti-Semitism and the Inquisition, which has also been entrusted to a commission, the Holy Father has carried on a great part of the re-examination of history on his own. For the most part, he has acted by himself and with a great deal of personal involvement, as is evidenced by the fact that most of his references to guilt and responsibility have been made during his travels, including the visit to Berlin in June of 1996, where he spoke of the lack of Catholic opposition to the Nazis, and at Vendée, France, in 1996, where he stated: "During those terrible battles [of the Catholic resistance to the French Revolution], many actions were marked by sin, both on the one side and on the other."

The historian, Albert Monticone once stated: "In this request for forgiveness we have the ultimate key to the travels of John Paul II." When the Pope speaks to a people, he recognizes the responsibility of those Catholics who had gone to that people before him. If he had not traveled, perhaps he would not have asked for forgiveness.

Pope John Paul II continues to travel and to ask forgiveness with a will that is stronger than his physical power, because he has taken upon himself a responsibility for the second millennium. He once confided that shortly after he was elected Pope, Cardinal Wyszynski said to him: "You must lead the Church into the third millennium." But he wants to do that less burdened by the weight of history, better reconciled with the other Christian communities, and with a bond of friendship with every religion and with all men of good will. And if that should cause some degree of confrontation with history, it will not be the end of the world. After all, he is a prophetic—as well as missionary—Pope.

PART ONE

Historical and Ecumenical Precedents

ONE

At One Time Nobody Asked for Forgiveness

Hans Urs von Balthasar wrote about "the burden of the dead." He was one of the theologians that Pope John Paul planned to make a cardinal and he was surely one of the most influential promoters of a "confession" of the sins committed by the Church throughout the centuries. The burden does not exist for other men and it is decidedly very light for Protestants, for they are not responsible for the first fifteen centuries of the Church. Neither is it a burden for the Orthodox Christians, who must answer only for their own particular Church.

But the Catholic has no escape. He would like "to make a new start and be as up to date as his peers," says von Balthasar, but he cannot free himself from the burden of the dead:

> The Catholic principle of Tradition (note the capital T) reminds him that the very Church he belongs to has done or allowed to be done things that we certainly can't approve of nowadays. Things that were not only permissible but even recommended under medieval popes seem, from the double perspective of Christ's own word and our present state of knowledge, absolutely

impermissible and even gravely sinful. They were obviously diametrically opposed to the spirit and word of Jesus.

Consequently, von Balthasar called for a full confession of sin. "The honest reaction is not only an immediate recognition of sinful responsibility but also a full one that will emphasize the harsh tragedy of the past." He then presented a list of some of the principal errors of the past:

> Forcible baptisms, inquisitions and *auto-da-fé's,* the St. Bartholomew's Day massacre, the conquest of new worlds with fire and sword as if the release of brutal exploitation were also the way of the religion of the cross and of love; unasked for and utterly absurd meddling in problems of developing natural science; proscriptions and excommunications by a spiritual authority which behaves as if it were political, and even demands recognition as such.[1]

There are three steps to the method proposed by von Balthasar: no defense can be given; it is necessary to make a full confession; it would not be right to throw stones "when no one is alive to stand up and plead for justification." All three steps have been observed throughout the long reign of Pope John Paul whenever he dealt with the "burden of the dead." In one of the ninety-four texts that refer to the errors of the past, there is even an explicit request not to throw stones. And in a discourse to the North American Indians at Phoenix, Arizona, on September 14, 1987, after admitting that Christians were responsible for the cultural oppression and injustices inflicted on the natives, he said: "But let us not dwell excessively on mistakes and wrongs, even as we commit ourselves to overcoming their present effects."

A radical theologian such as von Balthasar calls for a "full confession"; a courageous pope such as Wojtyla follows him almost literally; and public opinion not only approves but is grateful to him. Very few protested. But it was not always so. The idea of a full confession is something new, and previously it would have been opposed. At one time nobody in the Church ever asked for forgiveness.

The quotation from von Balthasar was written in 1965, the year of the close of the Second Vatican Council. It was also the year in which the young Bishop Wojtyla (45 years old) enthusiastically became involved in the "asking and giving of pardon" between the Polish and German bishops for the terrible struggle between the two nations which resulted in the genocide that took place in the Second World War. We shall speak of this in Chapter 7 of Part One.

It seems that during that period the "confession of sin" was the order of the day. Pope Paul VI had already asked for forgiveness from the separated brethren two years earlier, during the Second Vatican Council. The Fathers of the Council had done likewise in their decree on ecumenism (*Unitatis Redintegratio*, November, 1964). Relying on those firm declarations, Pope John Paul applied the "confession of sin" to a variety of situations, going far beyond the moderate list composed by von Balthasar. Then, thirty years later, he proposed the "examination of conscience" at the end of the second millennium, which we shall discuss in Chapters 8 and 9 of Part One. In the past ages of the Church, to whom could a pope turn for this confession of sin? Who among the popes had ever asked for forgiveness prior to Pope Paul VI?

Pope Adrian VI, whose pontificate lasted only 20 months (1522-1523), had been the last pope to confess the sins of the Church. He was also the last non-Italian pope of the Renaissance and the first "reforming" pope. His efforts to respond to the appeal of Luther for the reform of the Church were consistently blocked by the Roman Curia. He openly admitted the "abominable things" for which previous popes and their Curias were responsible.

The first explicit request for forgiveness after Pope Adrian VI is the one with which Pope Paul VI opened the second session of the Second Vatican Council in September of 1963. Prior to that, the apologetics of the Church did not permit any declaration of repentance; in fact, in 1832 Pope Gregory XVI declared that such a gesture is inadmissible. All in all, the resistance of the popes to any form of self-criticism lasted for 450 years, so it is no wonder that almost every declaration of Pope John Paul II on this topic provoked both applause and criticism.

Pope Adrian VI was known only to the specialists. It was Pope John Paul II who gave him an honorable mention. First of all, immediately after his own election in 1978, the Holy Father drew attention to the fact that he came from afar and, like his predecessor Adrian VI, who was born in Utrecht, Holland, he was non-Italian. Later, Pope John Paul frequently referred to Pope Adrian in order to substantiate his own requests for forgiveness. He called upon Adrian VI as his witness, together with the Second Vatican Council and Pope Paul VI. At least three times he quoted Pope Adrian in his meetings with Lutherans: at Mainz (1980), at Copenhagen (1989), and at Paderborn (1996).

Shortly after his election as pope, Adrian VI had sent Francesco Chieregati to Germany as his legate and commissioned him to separate the German princes from Luther, promising them the direct involvement of the papacy in the reform of the Church. According to the instructions received from the Pope on January 3, 1523, Chieregati was to read to the Diet of Nuremberg a text from Pope Adrian which admitted the fault of the Church for the continual postponement of the reform:

> We know well that even in this Holy See, until recently, abominable things have happened.... Therefore, it is not surprising that the malady has passed from the head to the members, from the Pope to the prelates. We intend to use all diligence to reform the Roman Curia, where all these evils began; then the recovery and renewal will start where the sickness had its origin. We feel all the more obligated to put these things in motion insofar as the whole world ardently desires such a reform.... But no one should be surprised that we are not eliminating all the abuses in one stroke. The sickness is, in fact, deeply rooted and has many symptoms. Consequently, it is necessary to proceed step by step, first applying the appropriate medicine to the more serious and more dangerous evils, in order not to cause even greater confusion by a hasty reform.[2]

The failure of this generous gesture by Pope Adrian seems to have convinced his successors that it was inopportune to own up to any responsibility. The specialists know of numerous passages in papal documents which for four centuries put them on their guard against any confession of sin. As an example we quote the most direct one and the best known, contained in the Encyclical *Mirari Vos,* promulgated by Pope Gregory XVI in 1832:

> It is evident how absurd and how insulting to the Church it is to propose a restoration and renewal as being necessary for advancing toward its salvation and its advancement, as if to infer that the Church could be subject to any defect or diminution or any other imperfection of a similar kind.[3]

To admit a defect or stain in the Church could lead to the suggestion of a reform; and since this would be very dangerous, it was felt necessary at all costs to avoid admitting any fault. Stated this way, it seems like a caricature. But this was precisely the attitude of the apologetics of the 1800's, which adhered faithfully to the directive of Pope Gregory XVI. We shall limit ourselves to one example among the many obvious ones, namely, the treatment of Blacks (which we shall treat in Part Two) as it is handled—and incredibly defended—in an interview in *Civiltà Cattolica* in 1865 under the title, *Il Concetto Morale della Schiavitù* (The Moral Concept of Slavery).[4]

For centuries the position of the papacy on the slave trade was not stated as clearly as one would have wanted it to be done. During the Civil War in the United States, slavery was at last condemned by European public opinion, greatly influenced by the novel, *Uncle Tom's Cabin*, and by the 1814-1815 Congress of Vienna (due in part to the pressure exercised by Pope Pius VII). And still, a Jesuit magazine tried to prove that *in se* and *per se* slavery was not contrary to the natural law as long as certain conditions were fulfilled. Consequently, one could not reproach those who made use of slavery where it was legal nor the popes who had not condemned it universally. In conclusion, it was stated that in treating the question of slavery, one should not amplify it beyond the limits assigned by the natural law. However, a person taken into slavery by deceit could not conclude that by reason of its teaching, the Church had participated in an evil deed.

Thus, for centuries there was no re-examination of history and any reappraisal called for by history was resisted in every way possible. When we discuss the case of Galileo in Part Two, we shall treat of the *Index of For-bidden Books*, where his *Dialogue on the Two Great World Systems* was listed for a long time.

A particular form of resisting the admission of er-rors of the past is exemplified in the confrontation with other Christian Churches; for example, the refusal of the Catholic Church to participate in the early phases of the ecumenical movement. If we look at the date of the birth of that movement, which coincides with the date of the Missionary Congress in Edinburgh in 1910, we discover that the Catholic Church joined the movement only a half century later, with the establishment of the Secretariat for Church Union in 1960 and the approval of the *Decree on Ecumenism* by the Second Vatican Coun-cil in 1964. As we shall see in the next Chapter, the long delay was due to the fear that the participation of the Catholic Church in the movement for church unity could be interpreted as an admission of responsibility for the division that needed mending.

TWO

The Protestants Were First

I n this Chapter we shall see that the "confession of sin" was first expressed by the Protestants, and for a long time the Catholic Church refused to do the same. Actually, the resistance coincides with the refusal of the papacy to take part in the ecumenical movement. We could also say that the confession of sin is the first and most important lesson that the papacy had to learn when it joined the ecumenical movement. We shall see that in advancing along this road, Pope John Paul at various times performs gestures or makes pronouncements that are contrary to some of his predecessors in this century. He sometimes does so (as when he pays homage to the pioneers of the ecumenical movement on entering their churches) with the explicit intention of reclaiming ground that had formerly been relinquished simply to avoid contacts that were considered dangerous.

That there is a sin of division for which all the churches are responsible was solemnly affirmed by the bishops of the Anglican Church in their Lambeth Conference in 1920. It is one of the first documents in the history of ecumenism in which a church admits its share of guilt:

> The causes of division lie deep in the past, and are by no means simple or wholly blameworthy. Yet none can doubt that self-will, ambition, and lack of charity among Christians have been principal factors in this complex process, and that these, together with blindness to the sin of disunion, are still mainly responsible for the breaches of Christendom. We acknowledge this condition of broken fellowship to be contrary to God's will, and we desire frankly to confess our share in the guilt of thus crippling the Body of Christ and hindering the activity of his Spirit.[5]

Seven years later, the conference, "Faith and Constitution," held at Lausanne in 1927, invited the participating churches (at last including representatives from the Orthodox churches) to look upon the divisions of the past with a spirit of repentance:

> One opinion maintains that no division of Christianity would have taken place without sin. Another opinion is that the divisions have been the inevitable result of the variety of spiritual gifts and the various interpretations of truth. Between these two is the opinion of those who look back at the divisions of the past in a spirit of repentance and sadness and with a lively sentiment of the divine mercy which, in spite of and perhaps through these divisions, has promoted the cause of God in the world.[6]

Roman Catholics had been invited to the conference at Lausanne, and two years before that, they had also been invited to a similar conference at Stockholm (1925) under the title of "Life and Action." In both instances the reply of the Catholic Church was negative. For all practical purposes, the two refusals became a statement of policy, influenced to a great extent by the Encyclical *Mortalium Animus* (1928) in which Pope Pius XI repeated the traditional invitation to the separated brethren to return "to the house of the Father, who will forget the injuries unjustly inflicted by them on the Apostolic See and will receive them with great love."

While the other churches were already admitting their responsibility, the Catholic Church was still pointing an accusing finger at their faults. Among the organizers of the conference on "Life and Action" at Stockholm was the Lutheran, Archbishop Söderblom of Uppsala, who had strongly urged the participation of Catholics. During a visit to Sweden in 1989, Pope John Paul II, in a spirit of remorse, laid flowers on the Archbishop's tomb in the Lutheran cathedral at Uppsala. Before that, at Edinburgh in June, 1982, he paid homage at the site where, in 1910, Anglican, Lutheran and Evangelical entities had participated in the Missionary Congress, from which Catholic representatives were naturally absent.

After the terrible events of the Second World War, the confession of sin in the ecumenical context became more urgent. This is the statement of the first ecumenical assembly of the World Council of Churches, held at Amsterdam in 1948:

> We come from Christian churches, which for a long time have been mutually misunderstood, ignored, and misrepresented; we come from countries that have been at war with each other; we are all sinners and heirs of the sins of our fathers. We have not corresponded with the blessing that God has bestowed on us.[7]

The same theme was further developed at the Second Assembly, held at Evanston, Illinois, in 1954:

God has also given us a new awareness of the sin that
characterizes the divided condition that we have inherited. In this life we shall never be able to escape from
our sinfulness, but we can repent of our sin when it has
been perceived. Also, when we have done what we have
thought it was right to do, we should remember that we
are culpably involved in sin—which is however not
entirely our doing—and that we cannot entirely dis-
sociate ourselves from the sin of division. The confession of union with Christ implies the confession of our
solidarity with our brothers in sin.... All of us should
be united, at least in looking with repentance at our division: not the repentance that we ought to look for
in others, but the repentance that we ourselves ought
to feel, cost what it may, even if others are not inclined
to imitate us. True repentance means to acknowledge
before God that we have sinned in such a way that we
have been ensnared in an evil from which we cannot
free ourselves, and as a result we cannot heal our division.[8]

Once again we can measure the degree of Catholic
and papal resistance to any confession of sin if we compare the preceding texts from the ecumenical assemblies
with the instruction from the Holy Office, published on
December 20, 1949: "Do not turn history against the
Catholics by exaggerating their faults, nor in favor of
the Reformers by concealing their faults. All things considered, that which constitutes the true essence of the
events is the defection from the Catholic faith."

THREE

Roncalli Corrects
the Liturgical Prayers

Pope John XXIII modified two liturgical prayers which were offensive to Jews and Muslims. It was tantamount to asking pardon for centuries-old offences. He wanted the Second Vatican Council to treat the separated brethren and the Jews differently, and he authorized Cardinal Bea to oversee the preparation of several important documents of the Council on these two topics.

The Jews

A beautiful book, *Perfidi Giudei Fratelli Maggiori* (Perfidious Jews, Elder Brothers), was written by the rabbi of Rome, Elio Toaff, who was a great ally of recent popes on the question of relations between Judaism and Catholicism.[9] The phrase "perfidious Jews" was the expression used by Catholics in the Good Friday liturgy until 1960; "elder brothers" was the expression used by Pope John Paul II when he visited the synagogue in Rome in April, 1986. The decision to change the prayer in the Good Friday liturgy is described by Cardinal Bea:

During the solemn liturgy on that day, on the spur of the moment, Pope John gave the order to omit from the well-known prayer for the Jews the troublesome adjective "perfidious," which today sounds very offensive, although in the Middle Ages, where it originated, it simply meant "non-believing." This gesture had a great effect on Jewish public opinion and it stirred up many hopes.[10]

To appreciate the full significance of Pope John's action, one need only recall how offensive the former prayer sounded to Jews, being held responsible for the death of Christ:

Let us pray also for the unbelieving Jews, that our Lord God would withdraw the veil from their hearts, that they also may acknowledge our Lord Jesus Christ.

Let us pray.
Almighty and everlasting God, who deny not your mercy even to the unbelieving Jews, hear our prayers, which we pour forth for the blindness of that people; that by acknowledging the light of your truth, which is Christ, they may be brought out of their darkness: through the same Lord.

The new prayer, introduced with the Missal of Pope Paul VI, is entirely different and seems to have come from another type of people:

Let us pray for the Jewish people, the first to hear the word of God, that they may continue to grow in the love of his name and in faithfulness to his covenant.

Let us pray.
Almighty and eternal God, long ago you gave your promise to Abraham and his posterity. Listen to your Church as we pray that the people you first made your own may arrive at the fullness of redemption.

The elimination of the words "unbelieving" and "blindness" are not the only liturgical innovations desired by Pope John XXIII in favor of the Jews. There was another offensive expression in the rite of baptism, and perhaps it was worse than the expressions in the Good Friday prayers. When a convert from Judaism was being baptized, the celebrant had to admonish the recipient to "abhor the Jewish perfidy." This phrase was abolished in 1960.

To understand the importance of the decision of Pope John XXIII, it is well to remember that the scandal of the expression "unbelieving Jews," which had become intolerable after the Holocaust (the *Sho'ah*), was noted during the reign of Pope Pius XII, but nothing was done about it. A rescript from the Congregation of Rites, dated June 10, 1948, explained that the Latin word *perfidia* meant only "lacking the faith." This was a terrible explanation as regards the Good Friday prayer, because it was precisely that Latin theological expression that had become an offensive term in the vernacular. It is an example of the influence of the rupture between Church and Synagogue with the rise of anti-Semitism.

The modification in that prayer captured the attention of a French Jew named Jules Isaac, a historian who had lost his wife and daughter in a concentration camp. He requested an audience with Pope John XXIII and was received on June 13, 1960. He submitted a memorandum concerning the feasibility of "a revision of the Christian teaching on the Jews" and the creation of "a sub-commission assigned to study the problem." The Pope told him that he had already been thinking about it, and when Isaac asked if he could count on "a speck of hope," the Pope responded: "You have the right to a great deal more than hope."

That meeting gave Pope John the idea that the Council should discuss the Jewish question. On September 18 he placed the matter in the hands of Cardinal Bea. Then, when presenting to the Council Fathers the text of Chapter 4 on ecumenism on November 19, 1963, the Cardinal could invoke the authority of Pope John XXIII, who had died five months earlier. He told them:

> Last year, in the month of December, I submitted in writing to the Sovereign Pontiff John XXIII of venerable memory the entire question *De Judaeis.* Only a few days later the Sovereign Pontiff informed me of his full approval.[11]

Separated Brethren

The re-examination of history by Pope John XXIII in regard to ecumenism began with the invitation to the separated brethren to send auditors to the Second Vatican Council and the creation of the Secretariat for Christian Unity (1960) so that it could suggest to the Council concrete methods of dialogue with a view to possible union. The maturation of Roncalli in ecumenical matters had taken place many years before. As early as 1926, when he was apostolic visitator at Sofia at the age of 45, he wrote to a young Orthodox Christian:

> Catholics and Orthodox are not enemies, but brothers. We have the same faith; we share in the same sacraments, and especially the Eucharist. We are divided by some disagreements concerning the divine constitution of the Church of Jesus Christ. The persons who were the cause of these disagreements have been dead for centuries. Let us abandon the old disputes and, each in his own domain, let us work to make our brothers good, by giving them good example. Later on, though

traveling along different paths, we shall achieve union among the churches to form together the true and unique Church of our Lord Jesus Christ.[12]

"Let us abandon the old disputes" is a concept that appears again and again in the texts of John Paul II that ask and offer pardon. But in addition to that, Pope John XXIII, because of his vast ecumenical experience before he was elected pope, had reached the conviction that a public self-criticism was necessary as regards the aggressive attitude of Catholics in confronting other Christians. This is how he spoke at a conference on the Catholic and Greek Orthodox Churches, held at Venice four years before he became pope:

> The pathway to the union of the various Christian confessions is charity, which is sometimes practiced little by one side or the other, and perhaps without malicious intentions. However, it results in very bad service to the Church and to souls.[13]

How much Roncalli has done as pope is known to all. We shall cite only a statement he made to Roger Schutz, the founder of the ecumenical community at Taizé: "We are not trying to find out who was wrong and who was right, but to reconcile ourselves to one another.... You are in the Church; be at peace." And when Schutz, whose evangelical community is open to Catholics and to everyone, exclaimed: "But then, we are Catholics!", the Holy Father said: "Yes; we are no longer separated."[14]

Islam

Yet another gesture of reconciliation, less well publicized but worthy of note, was made by Pope John XXIII to the world of Islam. He had learned to know and love the Islamic world during his years at Sofia and Istanbul. This gesture, like that toward the Jews, consisted of a change in the wording of the "Act of Consecration of the Human Race to the Sacred Heart of Jesus," which is normally recited each year on the last Sunday of October. On July 18, 1959, the Sacred Penitentiary suppressed the following sentence in the prayer: "Be Thou King of all those who are still involved in the darkness of idolatry or Islam."

Previously, on a visit to Algiers in 1950, when he was Nuncio at Paris, he had warmly greeted the vast throng of Arabs. This put Roncalli on the path that would lead to his successors' requests for pardon. By correcting the prayers concerning the Jews and Muslims, he took the first important step toward that which Pope John Paul II later called the purification of historical memory.

FOUR

Montini Asks and Offers Pardon

There are three pillars that support the central arch of the examination of conscience at the end of the millennium, with which the Catholic Church is occupied today:

— the "confession of sin" that came out of the assembly of the World Council of Churches, held at Amsterdam in 1948;

— Paul VI's petition for forgiveness from the separated brethren at the opening of the second session of the Second Vatican Council in September, 1963;

— the invitation of John Paul II to re-examine the history of the Church, contained in the memorandum sent to the cardinals in the spring of 1994.

These three occasions were marked by texts that are without a doubt among the most important Christian pronouncements of the last half century. One of them, which we shall discuss here, was by Pope Paul VI, and it is a summary of all his work for the re-examination of history. The document puts the Catholic Church at a level of the most mature ecumenical experience, makes a decisive contribution to the documents of the Second Vatican Council, and serves as the basis for the energetic launching of the initiative by Pope John Paul II more than thirty years later. This is the way Pope Paul VI spoke at St. Peter's on September 29, 1963, three months after his election:

> We speak now to the representatives of the Christian denominations separated from the Catholic Church, who have nevertheless been invited to take part as observers in this solemn assembly.... If we are in any way to blame for that separation, we humbly beg God's forgiveness and ask pardon too of our brethren who feel themselves to have been injured by us. For our part, we willingly forgive the injuries which the Catholic Church has suffered, and forget the grief endured during the long series of dissensions and separations.[15]

Twenty days later, on October 17, Pope Paul VI commented on his statement when he received the observer delegates in his private library. The comment is as important as the original announcement, because it states the reason for asking and giving pardon and the procedure to be followed:

> In our speech of September 29 we dared to have recourse first of all to Christian forgiveness, mutual if possible—*"veniam damus petimusque vicissim"* (let us forgive and ask for forgiveness mutually) [Horace]. Our minds need this tranquillity if they are to have friendly contacts and serene conversations. First of all, because it is Christian: "If then, in making your offering at the altar, you remember that your brother has something against you, leave there your offering in front of the altar and go first to reconcile yourself with your brother; then return and make the offering" (Mt 5:23-24).[16]

In that particular context the Pope's use of a quotation from the Latin poet Horace, together with a quotation from Christ, is worthy of note. It is a sign that even in its most modern representatives, which Montini certainly was, the papacy did not intend to distance itself from its humanistic tradition. But it also shows how strange a destiny some words can have. The words of Horace, which in verse 11 of the *Ars Poetica*—*Hanc veniam petimusque damusque vicissim*—refer to the tolerance of poetic license, are greatly ennobled by being quoted by the Pope. They will in fact become the maxim with which the Polish bishops will turn to the German bishops at the end of the Council for the reconciliation of the two peoples. They will also be the motto with which Pope John Paul II will repeatedly resume his indefatigable preaching of pardon, both in the ecumenical context and in that of international relations.

To emphasize the extent of the revolutionary announcement by Pope Paul VI, we shall cite yet another text from the beginning of his pontificate. It is from a discourse to the Roman Curia on September 21, 1963, concerning the need to accept criticism, however harsh, without polemical retaliation:

> We should accept the criticism that surrounds us with humility, with reflection, and even with gratitude. Rome does not need to defend itself by being deaf to the suggestions that come to it from honest voices, and much less if these voices are those of friends and brothers. To the accusations that are so often unfounded, response should surely be made, and also for the defense of its honor. But always without reluctance, without retaliation, and without controversy.

The request for pardon from our separated brethren, made by Pope Paul VI in the Council, prompted the assembly to formulate a similar text, which appeared in the first schema of the *Decree on the Catholic Eastern Churches,* but it was set aside because of the strong criticism that had been voiced in the first session of the Council in November, 1962. The criticism deserves to be looked at again because it is essentially no different from the criticism thirty-two years later, when Pope John Paul II proposed an examination of conscience at the end of the second millennium.

Cardinal Ruffini raised the question of the relationship between Christian sinners and the holiness of the Church, which was brought up again later by Cardinal Biffi. Ruffini asserted that it would be better to say that "some Christians" rather than "a part of the Church" were separated from the Church by schism. Bishop Franic of Yugoslavia put forth the classical distinction between the specific sins of individual Catholics and the general sin of those who fell away: "As regards the schism, the sins of Catholics were not extraneous from a historical point of view, but from a strictly theological perspective, only the others were guilty of the sin of schism; but we have remained faithful to the chair of Peter."

Bishop Pawlowski of Poland lamented the tendency to be "too quick to blame severely the Latin Church" and suggested that the same charity should be shown toward the Latin Church as was extended to the other churches. A similar protest was voiced by the Maronite, Bishop Khoury, who said that "it was an exaggeration to act as if only the Catholics are obliged to the mea culpa."

Moreover, the objection that no one has a right to accuse the dead, which was later raised against the proposal of Pope John Paul II, has ancient roots. It was expressed as follows by Bishop Velasco, OP, exiled bishop from Amoy, China: "It is sad that some members want to extract from the Council a statement on a very serious historical question, namely, the degree of responsibility of the Roman Church for the Eastern Schism. Such an accusation should be rejected. We should accuse ourselves and not the dead, who cannot defend themselves." Bishop Addazzi of Trani, Italy, stated that a humiliation of this sort is not fitting for the Council, neither for the past nor for the present: "It is not very honorable for a Council to condemn, even implicitly, the holy pontiffs who governed the Church at the time of the schism; we don't want the separated brethren to strike their breast in our presence, nor should we, who constitute the teaching Church, prostrate and humble ourselves before them."

After the pronouncement by Pope Paul VI, the resistance to the mea culpa was somewhat lessened. Those who were invited to make an examination of conscience were greatly encouraged and the debated text was rewritten in a more moderate form.

Having noted the support given by Pope Paul VI in the story of the Catholic mea culpa, we shall limit ourselves to a rapid survey of similar initiatives taken during his pontificate. We ought to mention the part he played in other references to self-examination by the Second Vatican Council.

Moreover, we should mention his visits to Jerusalem, Constantinople and Geneva, which are stages of reconciliation with the Jews and with other Christian churches. Also, as gestures signifying a reappraisal of history, we note the restoration of relics to various Eastern Churches and the return of the flag of Lepanto to Islam. Finally, the gift of the papal tiara for the poor also had a note of self-examination, and this time as a confrontation with Roman pomp and ceremony. We shall return to these ecumenical questions in Part Two.

We shall close with the account of a very significant gesture which took place during the Second Vatican Council, the effects of which could have a very beneficial influence in the years to come. It is the mutual lifting by Pope Paul VI and the Patriarch of Constantinople of the mutual excommunications of 1054. That act and the request for forgiveness, which took place on December 7, 1965, constituted the crowning of Pope Paul VI's work in the Second Vatican Council. He wanted to do it with a solemn pronouncement that would serve as an example and a norm for future ceremonies of that type, especially since former pontiffs had issued many excommunications that no pope today could approve:

> Pope Paul VI and Patriarch Athenagoras I with his synod, in common agreement, declare that:
>
> A. They regret the offensive words, the reproaches without foundation, and the reprehensible gestures which, on both sides, have marked or accompanied the sad events of this period.
>
> B. They likewise regret and remove both from memory and from the midst of the Church the sentences of excommunication which followed these events, the memory of which has influenced actions up to our own day and has hindered closer relations in charity; and they commit these excommunications to oblivion.[17]

This great gesture was followed by two lesser ones that indicated the personal commitment of both prelates to the restoration of lost fellowship: the kiss of peace exchanged with the Patriarch Athenagoras at Jerusalem on January 6, 1964, and the kissing of the foot of the delegate from Constantinople on the tenth anniversary of the mutual lifting of excommunication. Pope Paul VI characterized the kiss of peace exchanged with Athenagoras as "a symbol and an example of the charity which, breaking with the past, is ready to forgive."

Even more constructive was the gesture in St. Peter's on December 14, 1975, marking the tenth anniversary of the reconciliation with Constantinople. Dressed in liturgical vestments, Pope Paul suddenly knelt and kissed the foot of Melitone, the Metropolitan who had been sent as the representative of the Patriarch of Constantinople. That kiss of the Metropolitan's slipper was a remarkable gesture; it went beyond a symbol and erased an ancient breach of trust. Pope Paul wanted it to be "an act of reparation for the contrary behavior of his predecessor Eugene IV at his meeting with the Patriarch Joseph II at the Council of Ferrara-Florence."

Even apart from the Conciliar and ecumenical setting, Pope Paul undertook a re-examination of history and asked for forgiveness. For example, in a memorable discourse in the Sistine Chapel, he asked pardon of artists for the lack of understanding on the part of the Church in past centuries.

Pope Paul possessed an instinctive humility which enabled him to understand other people's reasons and to treat them fairly at the first meeting. Even before he was elected to the papacy, Montini had the idea that the Church should ask for forgiveness from its brothers as well as from God (and on one occasion he said "before" asking forgiveness from God). Even as Archbishop of Milan he had already used the request for forgiveness as a last attempt to be listened to, where there was no tradition of dialogue. For example, on opening the "Great Mission for Milan" on November 10, 1957, he asked for forgiveness "in a friendly manner" of those who had distanced themselves from the Church:

> If a voice could reach you, my absent sons, the first would be one that asks forgiveness in a friendly manner. Yes; we ask you, before we ask God.... If we have not understood you, and if we have too easily ignored you; if we have not taken care of you; if we have not been good masters of the spiritual life and physicians of souls; if we have not been able to speak to you about God as we should have done; if we have treated you with aloofness, with derision, with controversy, today we ask your forgiveness.[18]

FIVE

The Council Follows the Pope

With the coming of the Second Vatican Council, the Catholic Church began to speak in ecumenical terms about the confession of sin and the request for forgiveness. The most impressive text is contained in the *Decree on Ecumenism,* promulgated on November 21, 1964. We have already seen the decisive role played by Pope Paul VI, who had anticipated the confession of sin and encouraged the Council to take that step. Perhaps it was inevitable that the Catholic Church should be guided by a pope to admit its historical responsibility, since for many centuries there had been so many popes who had silenced every voice that dared to suggest any such responsibility.

Here is the central confession of the Second Vatican Council, contained in the *Decree on Ecumenism,* to which Pope Paul VI habitually referred when speaking of the need to ask for forgiveness:

> St. John has testified: "If we say we have not sinned, we make him a liar, and his word is not in us" (1 Jn 1:10). This holds good for sins against unity. Thus, in humble prayer we beg pardon of God and of our separated brethren, just as we forgive them that offend us (*Unitatis Redintegratio,* 7).

There is yet another passage in the document on ecumenism that makes reference to the sin of division among the churches and this was also quoted by Pope Paul VI:

> In this one and only Church of God from its very beginnings there arose certain rifts, which the Apostle strongly censures as damnable. But in subsequent centuries much more serious dissensions appeared and large communities became separated from full communion with the Catholic Church—for which, often enough, men of both sides were to blame (*Ibid.,* 3).

The Church of Vatican II was able to confess its faults and ask forgiveness because it admitted that it was at once both holy and sinful, as is evident in this passage from the *Dogmatic Constitution on the Church* (November 21, 1964):

> Christ, "holy, innocent and undefiled" (Heb 7:26), knew nothing of sin (2 Cor 5:21), but came only to expiate the sins of the people (Heb 2:17). The Church, however, clasping sinners to her bosom, at once holy and always in need of purification, follows constantly the path of penance and renewal (*Lumen Gentium,* 8).

This text is as important as the one from the document on ecumenism, which asks forgiveness from the separated brethren. In one single statement it presents the twofold vision of the Church as "holy in Christ" and "sinful in its members." Both of these sentiments were conjoined in the patristic and medieval periods but separated in the division between the Protestant Reformation and the Catholic Counter-Reformation. This prompted the Protestants to accentuate the denunciation of sin in the Church and the Catholics to rally to the defense of the holiness of the Church.

The discussions during the Council that led to the approval of this text have been revived recently, since Pope John Paul II proposed the idea of an examination of conscience at the end of this millennium. At the moment it has reached a state of linguistic compromise to which the Pope also adheres: fault and sin are attributed to the "sons of the Church" but never directly to the Church, even when treating of officials of the Church or the Church's organisms, to which faults are occasionally attributed.

The Vatican has admitted the responsibility of the Church for the persecution of the Jews, for violations of religious freedom, and for the case of Galileo. Later on we shall report on the developments, but we must insist at the outset that the confessions of fault are inadequate and are so considered by Pope John Paul II. He has repeatedly returned to these cases, as we shall see when we come to the pertinent chapters in Part Two.

As regards anti-Semitism, the admission of Catholic responsibility is implicit in the *Declaration on the Relation of the Church to Non-Christian Religions* (October 28, 1965), which deplores such manifestations coming "from any source," and therefore including the Church. But it is not very much, and when we treat in particular of the Jews, we shall see that an explicit request for forgiveness has not yet been made, although it is more than thirty years since the admission of responsibility by the Second Vatican Council:

> Indeed, the Church reproves every form of persecution against whomsoever it may be directed. Remembering, then, her common heritage with the Jews and moved not by any political consideration, but solely by the religious motivation of Christian charity, she deplores all hatreds, persecutions, displays of anti-

Semitism leveled at any time or from any source against the Jews (*Nostra Aetate*, 4).

The following passage from the *Declaration on Religious Liberty* (December 7, 1965) will receive flesh and blood from the pronouncements of Pope John Paul II concerning the religious wars, the Inquisition and Integralism (an extreme form of dogmatic vigilantism characterized by the uncompromising conviction that the Roman Catholic Church, and it alone, possesses the whole truth: tr.):

> Although in the life of the people of God in its pilgrimage through the vicissitudes of human history there has at times appeared a form of behavior which was hardly in keeping with the spirit of the Gospel and was even opposed to it, it has always remained the teaching of the Church that no one is to be coerced into believing (*Dignitatis Humanae*, 12).

Pope John Paul will also have much to say about Galileo, whom the Council does not mention by name, but refers to him in this passage from the *Pastoral Constitution on the Church in the Modern World* (December 7, 1965):

> We cannot but deplore certain attitudes (not unknown among Christians) deriving from a shortsighted view of the rightful autonomy of science; they have occasioned conflict and controversy and have misled many into opposing faith and science (*Gaudium et Spes*, 36).

But over and above this timid reference to Galileo, the document does contain numerous other passages of self-criticism based on the experience of the Church, whether on a specific topic such as religious life or the Church's social involvement:

For atheism, taken as a whole, is not present in the mind of man from the start. It springs from various causes, among which must be included a critical reaction against religions and, in some places, against the Christian religion in particular. Believers can thus have more than a little to do with the rise of atheism. To the extent that they are careless about their instruction in the faith, or present its teaching falsely, or even fail in their religious, moral and social life, they must be said to conceal rather than reveal the true nature of God and of religion.... By the power of the Holy Spirit the Church is the faithful spouse of the Lord and will never fail to be a sign of salvation in the world; but it is by no means unaware that down through the centuries there have been among its members, both clerical and lay, some who were disloyal to the Spirit of God. Today as well the Church is not blind to the discrepancy between the message it proclaims and the human weakness of those to whom the Gospel has been entrusted. Whatever is history's judgment on these shortcomings, we cannot ignore them and we must combat them earnestly, lest they hinder the spread of the Gospel (*Gaudium et Spes,* 19 and 43).

The admission of the Council appears only for a moment, but even then it was too much for some. Nevertheless, a little more than ten years after the promulgation of *Gaudium et Spes,* it was considered insufficient by the Vatican and even more so by the new Pope. Moreover, the admission of fault by the Council was a disappointment to the ecumenical observers. We shall limit ourselves to the most authoritative voice among them, that of Karl Barth. His dissatisfaction with the mea culpa of Vatican Council II is especially significant because it is found in a book in which he expresses his great appreciation for the Council and uses the term

"Evangelical-Catholic" to describe himself. The book is called *Ad Limina Apostolorum* and it was written in 1967, on his return from a trip to Rome, where he met with Pope Paul VI and various members of the Curia as well as several outstanding Catholic theologians.

There are three passages in the book in which Barth laments the lack of an explicit confession of sin in the documents of Vatican II. First and foremost, regarding the Jews, he says: "Would it not be more appropriate, in view of the anti-Semitism of the ancient, the medieval, and to a large extent the modern Church, to set forth an explicit confession of guilt here, rather than in respect to the separated brethren?"

As regards the Muslims, whom the Conciliar document *Nostra Aetate* mentions explicitly, "would not such a confession be appropriate in view of the deplorable role of the Church in the so-called Crusades?!" (It is Barth who ended the question with a question mark as well as an exclamation point, as if to tell us that it is more than obvious!)

Finally, concerning the *Declaration on Religious Liberty*, which, according to Barth, "demands from governments the free scope due Christians and the Church for the confirmation and spreading of their faith," he has this to say: "Is it legitimate for the Church (and not only the Catholic Church) to make this demand in view of the extensive periods of her history which were dominated by her pact with the state through *'cogite intrare'* ('force them to come in,' Lk 14:23)? Would not a rather comprehensive confession of guilt be more appropriate here?"

The spirit in which Karl Barth formulated these inquiries is evident from a fourth logical question concerning the document on ecumenism: since the ecumenical movement arose outside the Catholic Church, and Catholics are now at last called to participate in it, "why is this initiative of the non-Catholic churches not explicitly recognized?"[19]

Up to this time only two of the questions addressed to Rome by Karl Barth have been answered, and precisely by Pope John Paul II: the questions on ecumenism and on religious liberty. In the Encyclical *Ut Unum Sint,* 7, he explicitly acknowledges the role of the Protestants and the Orthodox in the ecumenical movement; and he had already confessed the "sin" against religious liberty in his discourse to the European parliament in 1988. Nevertheless, as I have already stated, an explicit confession of sin has not yet been made concerning Islam and Judaism. What Pope John Paul has said up to now is only a prelude to that which ought to be said.

SIX

Luciani Had a Program

Luciani was Pope for only thirty-three days, and he did not say a single word about the need to revise the history of the Church. However, he did perform an act that was very significant and important: he renounced the papal tiara and replaced the coronation ceremony with a simple celebration of the beginning of his pontificate.

Although we do not have any particular statements by him concerning the re-examination of history, we do have many other statements attributed to him. Unfortunately, none of them are direct quotations or first-hand testimony. Nevertheless, they deserve to be reported, because they do tell us something about the way he looked at the future immediately after his election. Moreover, they are in a sense a preview of many of the initiatives that would be taken later by Pope John Paul II. They are a compilation of things that were discussed with him or thought by those around him and then made known to him.

My source for this information about the plans of Pope Luciani (I repeat, an indirect and secondary source, but the only one available) is a journalist from Venice named Camillo Bassotto, director of the international film festival held at Venice. He has written a book about Pope Luciani, entitled *Il Mio Cuore é Ancora a Venezia* (My Heart Is Still in Venice). It contains two lengthy sections on projects that were envisioned for the pontificate of Pope John Paul I, based on the testimony of two persons who were directly involved in discussions with the Pope, one of whom is deceased and the other remains anonymous.

The first was Germano Pattaro, a priest of Venice and a great promoter of ecumenism, who died in December, 1986. He had been called to Rome shortly after the papal election and Pope John Paul I had three conversations with him in which he sought help and advice concerning the projects of his pontificate. Bassotto claims to have received from Father Pattaro a lengthy oral report of his discussions with the Pope and a shorter written account. Bassotto has used the two reports interchangeably, without identifying one or the other. To this day, as far as anyone knows, the written material has not been published or consigned to any public archive.

The second testimony was given to Bassotto in writing by "a Roman ecclesiastic" who had asked not to be identified. He claims to have received confidential material directly from Pope Luciani. His testimony is much more sober in tone than that of Father Pattaro, but both accounts are substantially in agreement. When I asked for the identity of the Roman ecclesiastic and requested a copy of the original written testimony, Bassotto replied that it is not yet the time to release it.

I shall quote some of the confidential material attributed to Pope Luciani, as related in the book by Bassotto,

giving preference to material that has any connection
with the mea culpa's of Pope Wojtyla. The quotations
are all attributed to Pope John Paul I and arranged under the same headings as are listed in Part Two of this
book, and I have placed in italics the statements that
correspond more directly with pronouncements made
later by Pope Wojtyla after the publication of the book
by Camillo Bassotto.

Divisions between the Churches

"We must revise in depth the attitude and opinion
we have had for centuries concerning the brethren of
the Christian churches. For a long time we have not
searched with sufficient tenacity and charity, with fore-
sight and trust and humility, the way to unity, without
taking away anything from the essence, the roots and
the patrimony of our own faith. Jesus tells us: 'By this
they shall know that you are my disciples: if you love
one another as I have loved you.' We have not loved one
another. For centuries we have ignored and attacked
one another. All the Christian churches, including ourselves, have sinned against love and against the command of Christ.... I know that the division of Christians
is a sin and that the unity of Christians is a gift of God.
*There will never be true ecumenism if we do not do penance; if
we do not exchange peace and pardon; if we are not converted.
We have sinned. Every ecumenical action should be an act of
'reconciliation' performed with repentance and humility.* As
long as we are here on earth, we shall be sinners. The
Church, 'holy and immaculate, without stain or wrinkle'
(Eph 5:27), is the Church of the promise, which Christ
will bring to full completion only on the day of judgment and not before" (Bassotto, pp. 135, 144, 233).

Women

"The prejudice against women is strong now throughout all society. In the Church the pope should speak a clear, firm and definitive word on the dignity, equality, merit, rights, value and mission of women. Following the example of Jesus, *the pope should reaffirm the proper place that belongs to women in the community of men and in the ecclesiastical community, as indicated by the Council*" (pp. 143, 234).

The Jews

"If Christ the Lord gives me life; if I have the strength, enlightenment and support, I plan to call together a representation of bishops from all over the world for an act of repentance, humility, reparation, peace and love of the universal Church, to be repeated each year by the pope and by bishops of the local churches on Good Friday. We Christians have sinned against the Jews, our brothers in God and in Abraham; we have ignored and maligned them for centuries.... In Jesus' name we ought to make peace forever with the Jews. We have already made some progress along the path of Judaeo-Christian dialogue, but there are still so many shadows hovering over the centuries. It is necessary that the manifestation of good intentions, clarity of ideas, humility and good will should continue. It took the extermination camps of the Nazis to awaken the conscience of humanity and of Christians in regard to the Jews. The Holocaust is also a religious matter. The Jews were also killed for their religion. The thought and attitude of the Church toward Jews have changed profoundly. We should enlighten Christians and urge priests and bishops to speak clearly and openly. We

Christians still have much to learn about the facts and the history of the Jewish people. We should eliminate from Good Friday the anti-Jewish references that have endured for almost two thousand years. Pope John XXIII has already done something, but it is necessary to do more. Let us not forget that the two words 'Good Friday' still resound in the ears of older Jews all over the world as a sad and sometimes tragic remembrance of the events that took place on that day. It should be a day of peace and brotherhood, of repentance and silence, on which all men are called to acknowledge the infinite mercy of God" (pp. 134-135).

Indians and Blacks

"I want to tell you another thought of mine that evolved after my first trips to Africa and Latin America. *At some moments in history, we Christians have been tolerant of the massacre of Indians, racism and the deportation of people from Africa.* It has been said that fifty million Blacks were forcefully carried off as slaves from Africa to America. Even then there were courageous men who cried out against the scandal and the sin. I know of one: the Dominican, Las Casas, who was not listened to but was persecuted. His denunciations of the genocide of those people were not heeded by the Christian community of that time, so they were not prompted to come to the defense of those innocent people. With David we should say to the Lord: 'I acknowledged my sin to you, my guilt I covered not. I said: "I confess my faults to the Lord," and you took away the guilt of my sin' (Ps 32:5). *To confess the historical faults of the Church is a sign of humility and truth, a sign of hope for a better future.* For two thousand years the only gauge of a Christian is love and the

Gospel of Christ the Lord. *It has been said that one cannot judge the events of those times with today's sensibility. But it is not a question of sensibility; it is a question of truth.* The Church is the critical conscience of today and of yesterday. The Church must recapture its prophetic power. Its evangelical yes and no, in the light of day and in sight of everyone."

The Inquisition

"Acknowledging that it is a sinner in its members and in its institutions, the Church humbly deplores the difficult and painful moments of its passage through history, as in the case of the Inquisition and the very sad times of the temporal power of the popes. We should not be afraid to confess our sin.... I would like the Congregation for the Doctrine of the Faith to get rid of that flavor and zeal of the Inquisition that still remains in it.... *The Inquisition has left moral wounds that are not yet healed.* Charity is the mother of justice and of truth" (pp. 135, 239).

Martyrs of the East

"As Pastor of the universal Church, I want to remember and honor the bishops, priests, religious and Christians who, in Soviet Russia, in the countries of Eastern Europe, in the Baltic nations and in other countries, are living in the catacombs and are suffering for Jesus Christ.... *We have forgotten too soon these witnesses to Christ who have inscribed their suffering in the Christian martyrology.* I intend to do so out of a purely religious spirit. I know that it could stir up some buried 'sentiments,' but we cannot remain silent. Too much diplomacy can sometimes become pure craftiness, and this is not in the spirit of the Church" (pp. 244-245).

Rehabilitation

Pope Luciani spoke at length with Father Pattaro about four ecclesiastics who have left proof of their love for the Church: Antonio Rosmini, Cardinal Andrea Ferrari (later proclaimed Blessed by Pope John Paul II), Lorenzo Milani and Primo Mazzolari. Concerning the suspicions of Pope St. Pius X about Cardinal Ferrari, Pope Luciani said: "You know that even the saints can make mistakes." Concerning Milani and Mazzolari, he said: "I am indebted to both of them; I knew them personally. They gave proof of their love for their bishops and for the Church. Two priests, two pastors, two prophets who were abandoned." Again: "We priests, we bishops, firm in our Quietism, have not understood that these men saw clearly, they saw correctly, and they saw from a distance." Pope Luciani planned to honor Milani and Mazzolari ("They deserve to receive the honor and the position that belongs to them in the Church"). He also wanted to rehabilitate Rosmini, who had been condemned by the Holy Office (pp. 129-131, passim).

History of the Papacy

"In my travels I would want everything to be done with simplicity and charity. Jesus Christ, Peter and Paul and John were not heads of state. I know and understand all the historical reasons, from tradition and from the desire to give prestige to the Church and the pope, and of being a help to the people where Christians live. But how can one change his life in an instant, don a completely different garb, assume a title and an authority intrinsically different from that of a bishop or pastor, such as that of 'Sovereign of the city of Rome'? I know very well that I will not be the one to change the rules established for centuries, but the Church should not have power nor possess wealth.... I don't want escorts or soldiers. I do not want the Swiss Guard to kneel when I pass by or anyone else to do so either" (p. 127).

Titles of the Pope

"During these days I was curious to read in the *Annuario Pontificio* the titles that are conferred on the pope: 'John Paul I, Bishop of Rome, Vicar of Christ, Successor of the Prince of the Apostles, Sovereign Pontiff of the Universal Church, Patriarch of the West, Primate of Italy, Metropolitan Archbishop of the Roman Province, Sovereign of the State of Vatican City, Servant of the Servants of God.' It is a heritage of temporal power. The only thing missing is: the Pope the King. The true titles ought to be: ...elected Bishop of Rome and hence Successor of the Apostle Peter and therefore Servant of the Servants of God. How could the pope present himself and dialogue with the sister churches as a brother and father in Christ when invested with all those titles?... I have the impression that the figure of the pope is praised too much. There is the danger of falling into the cult of the personality, which I absolutely do not want.... A little more than a hundred years have passed since the decline of the temporal power of the popes; otherwise I too would now be a pope-king, with an army of soldiers and perhaps a police force to protect the goods, the lands and the palaces of the popes. How beautiful it would have been if the pope had himself voluntarily renounced all temporal power! He should have done it first. Let us give thanks to the Lord who has willed it and has done it" (pp. 233, 236, 248).

SEVEN

The Advantage of a Polish Pope

Without the Second Vatican Council there would not have been the mea culpa's of Pope John Paul II. And if the Pope had not traveled, the mea culpa's would not have been so numerous. On the other hand, the examination of conscience at the end of the millennium, which is truly an original idea of this Pope, and is worth more than all the mea culpa's taken together, would never have been proposed without the experience of failure, especially the ecumenical failure in the East, which occurred shortly after the fall of Communism. But first there was Poland.

The Polish element is present in this ecumenical context of the pontificate of John Paul II. We shall call it the advantage of the Polish Pope over the infinite number of Italian popes, which is something that predisposed the first Slav Pope in history to have greater freedom in rendering an account of the history of the papacy. He was much less under the weight of that history. And this was true first of all by reason of his having been geographically marginalized in the Church. There were no Poles in the Crusades, among the Grand Inquisitors, the judges of Galileo, the oppressors of the

Indians in the Americas, or the kidnappers of the Blacks in Africa.

Moreover, on a positive note, there is something Polish in the ease with which John Paul II has shown that he knows how to react to the "burden of the dead," to use the phrase of von Balthasar. In Poland there was no Counter-Reformation, accompanied by repression and a military search for Protestants. Freedom of conscience had been proclaimed there before any other place in Europe. And there was no conflict between the Church and nationalism or between the Church and the laity.[20]

Finally, there was no case like that of Galileo in Polish history. It is difficult to explain why in a few words; it is easier to do it with a poem by Karol Wojtyla in praise of Copernicus, the Galileo of Poland, of whom the Church has always been proud:

> We walk on seams.
> Earth once appeared even, smooth.
> For generations they thought her flat disc was
> surrounded by water below and the sun above.
> And Copernicus came: earth lost its hinges,
> it now became hinged on motion.
> We walk on the seams not as before
> (Copernicus stopped the sun and gave the earth
> a push).[21]

Copernicus is described in biblical terms, with the words which the Bible puts in the mouth of Joshua and were used to condemn Galileo. Among us, only someone who was anticlerical could speak that way about Galileo, but in Poland the future Pope spoke that way on the vigil of becoming a cardinal. Then, in 1973, Cardinal Wojtyla, Archbishop of Krakow, presided over the Committee of the Polish episcopate for the celebration of the five hundredth anniversary of the birth of Nikolaj Kopernik (Copernicus), a Polish priest who ministered to the sick poor and dedicated his scientific work on the heavenly spheres to Pope Paul III.[22]

For the centenary celebration, Cardinal Wojtyla delivered an address at the theological faculty of Krakow, entitled "Science, a Good for the Nation, the Church and Humanity." In it he vindicated Copernicus as a glory of the Church.[23]

With this sentiment of laudable pride in what the Church had done for science (without any of the complication that had always characterized the Italian clergy), shortly after being elected Pope, dissatisfied with the way the Second Vatican Council had treated the question, he turned to the Galileo case in order to clarify that "grievous misunderstanding." And the Galileo case would be followed by other re-examinations of history.

After Poland, the Council. The young Bishop Wojtyla was greatly impressed by Pope Paul's request for forgiveness from the separated brethren at the opening of the second session of the Second Vatican Council in September of 1963. Since then, he has frequently referred to that statement. For example, in his Encyclical, *Ut Unum Sint*, he said: "I join my Predecessor Paul VI in asking forgiveness" (88). Actually, most of his requests for forgiveness are in the field of ecumenism.

During the Council, the young Wojtyla had also been deeply moved by the words of Cardinal Beran of Prague, who spoke about the *Declaration on Religious Liberty* at the last session.

The Cardinal stated that "in my country, the Catholic Church at this time seems to be suffering expiation for defects and sins committed in her name in times gone by against religious liberty." He recalled the sins committed in the name of the Church, not only in the execution of the priest, Jan Hus, but also in the forced reconversion of the Czech people to the Catholic faith by the application of the principle *cuius regio eius religio* (the people of a territory must follow the religion of their ruler). Cardinal Beran then said that "in this Council the principle of religious liberty and freedom of conscience must be enunciated in very clear words and without any restrictions.... If we do this, even in the spirit of penance for such sins of the past, the moral authority of our Church will be greatly augmented for the benefit of the world."[24] The stirring message from Cardinal Beran was recalled by Pope John Paul II when he visited Prague on April 21, 1990. Actually, Cardinal Beran's speech contained all the elements necessary for an examination of conscience at the end of the millennium, and Archbishop Wojtyla never forgot it.

Even more important in the ecumenical context was the participation of Archbishop Wojtyla in the gesture of reconciliation between the Polish and German bishops. That was a decisive stage in the development of his conviction of the need for a continual re-examination of the history of the Church and the restoration and implementation of the Gospel teaching. It marks his attainment of ecumenical maturity even before the beginning of his pontificate.

Wojtyla had been a member of the delegation of the Polish episcopate that met with the German delegation in September of 1978. The visit took place at Mainz on September 27, some twenty days before the white smoke announced the election of a new pope. The theme of the document on reconciliation was "Forgive and Ask Forgiveness." It is a phrase which Wojtyla borrowed from Pope Paul VI and one which would become the password in his proposal for the events marking the end of the millennium. The same theme of forgiveness is found in the European Synod of 1991, the preparatory texts for the Great Jubilee, the appeal for peace in the former Yugoslavia in September, 1994 (when he was unable to visit Sarajevo and Zagreb), and in the ecumenical documents promulgated in 1995.

The initiative for reconciliation was taken at the end of the Second Vatican Council by the Polish bishops to mark the millennium of the conversion of Poland (966-1966). The letter of the Polish bishops to the German bishops in November, 1965, is an invitation to reciprocal forgiveness, covering the entire history of the two peoples, but especially for the events of the Second World War, so that it would be possible to celebrate the millennium of Poland's conversion "with a tranquil conscience."

The letter recalls the Nazi occupation of Poland, the extermination of "six million Polish citizens, most of whom were of Jewish extraction," and the persecution of the Church. "Two thousand priests and five bishops (a quarter of the episcopate at that time) were killed in the concentration camps; hundreds of priests and tens of thousands from the civilian population were shot on the spot at the very beginning of the occupation." Then follows the invitation to dialogue and forgiveness:

> In spite of all this, in spite of the fact that the weight of the past makes the present situation seem desperate, precisely because of that, Reverend Brothers, we send out an appeal: Let us try to forget! No polemics; no continuation of the cold war, but the beginning of a dialogue.... In this very Christian and at the same time very human spirit, we extend our hands to you, seated on the benches of a Council that is about to end, forgiving and asking forgiveness.

"With emotion and joy" the German bishops grasped the hands extended by the Poles and they responded on December 5, 1965:

> We also ask you to forget; we ask you to forgive. To forget is human. The request for forgiveness is an invitation to one who has suffered an injustice to look with the merciful eyes of God and to let us begin anew.

There was peace between the two Catholic communities, but the Polish Communist government instigated a war of propaganda against the Polish episcopate, concentrating especially on Cardinal Wyszynski and Archbishop Wojtyla. The object of the invective was precisely the phrase "forgiving and asking forgiveness." The Communist response was: "We shall not forget and we shall not forgive." The workers of the Solvay establishment expressed their indignation in a letter to Archbishop Wojtyla, who had worked there as a laborer during the war.

The Archbishop responded in the Polish journal, *Dziennik Polski* on May 13, 1966, but they replied that Poland has nothing for which to ask forgiveness. Previously, on March 7, the Prime Minister had protested in an interview because the Polish bishops had forgiven the Germans for all the crimes committed against Poland, "including the crime of genocide, without any request for forgiveness having come from the Germans." The official response of the episcopate to this protest was contained in a letter dated February 10, 1966, and it is written in the style typical of Wojtyla:

> If after a thousand years we must live close together, which is difficult and bitter for us, it has been possible only by following the path of mutual understanding. Does the Polish nation have reason to ask forgiveness

from its neighbors? Certainly not. We are convinced that during the centuries we as a nation have not committed any wrongs politically, economically or culturally against the German nation. But we also acknowledge the Christian principle, which has also been emphasized in recent literary works, that "there are no innocents" (Albert Camus). We are convinced that if only one unworthy Pole could be found who during the centuries of our history had committed just one unworthy action, that would be enough to say: we ask for forgiveness.

The process of reconciliation between the two episcopates culminated in the visit of a Polish delegation to their German colleagues in September, 1978. Cardinal Wojtyla delivered two discourses at Fulda; one of which was to the Conference of German Bishops, and a third discourse at Cologne. During a homily at the cathedral in Fulda on September 22, he stated that this meeting had "reinforced" the two churches "in truth and in love" and, at the moment when the second millennium is drawing to a close, it has helped "to heal the wounds of the past, both ancient and more recent."

To verify that the masterful hand of Wojtyla was involved both in the documents issued between 1965 and 1966, and in the meetings in 1978, we can refer to the call to reconciliation proposed by Pope John Paul II in one of the most dramatic texts of his pontificate. I am referring to the homily for peace in the Balkans, delivered at Castel Gandolfo on September 8, 1994, the very day on which he had wanted to visit the city of Sarajevo:

> The history of mankind, of peoples and nations, is charged with mutual resentment and injustice. How important were the historical words addressed by the Polish bishops to their German confrères at the end of the Second Vatican Council: "We forgive and we ask

forgiveness." If in that region of Europe peace was possible, it would seem to have come about precisely because of the attitude expressed in those words (*L'Osservatore Romano* [English Edition], September 8, 1994).

In addition to Poland and the Council, the travels of Pope John Paul II gave him ample opportunity to ask for forgiveness because he had the opportunity to meet people who had experienced injustices in the past. It was in his travels that a tone of self-criticism was first evident when he referred to the division of the churches (1980); the Inquisition (1982); relations with Islam (1982); Catholic responsibility in wars (1983); the Mafia (1983); the treatment of Indians (1984) and of the Blacks (1985); religious wars and persecution (1988); the Eastern Schism (1991). It was also during his travels that he first spoke of the need to purge the memory of history and admit responsibility and fault (1980); leading up to reciprocal forgiveness (1983). It was again during his travels that he reviewed the judgment of history on Luther (1980), Calvin and Zwingli (1984), and Hus (1990). Shorter trips took him to the Lutheran church in Rome (1983) and the Jewish synagogue in Rome (1986), which prompted him to acknowledge the repression of religious minorities in Rome up until the last century.

Predisposed by his Polish experience and the Second Vatican Council, and stimulated by his contacts with people during his travels, Pope John Paul had already compiled a vast historical re-evaluation of particular topics when the harsh experience of failure in ecumenical relations prompted him to suggest an examination of conscience at the end of the second millennium. It is his original contribution in this area. He made the proposal in a memorandum that he sent to the cardinals in the spring of 1994, but the idea had already matured by 1991. The first public statement was published in the Italian newspaper, *La Stampa,* November 2, 1993, reporting an interview by Jas Gawronski:

> At the end of this second millennium we must make an examination of conscience: where we are, where Christ has brought us, where we have deviated from the Gospel.

EIGHT

Opposition from the Cardinals

It is only a "work sheet," and yet it could be the most important document of Pope John Paul II's pontificate. I am referring to the memorandum sent to the cardinals in the spring of 1994. It is not known who could have drawn it up. Neither is the precise date known. It was sent to the cardinals attending an Extraordinary Consistory and it reached the newspapers through a news leak. All the cardinals received it and studied it, but it was never officially published. Nevertheless, on two occasions during the Consistory, Pope John Paul claimed that he was the author: "As I pointed out in the memorandum" and "In the cited memorandum I have emphasized."

Consequently, it is a text by the Pope. Perhaps he himself did not write it, since he does not write a great deal of what he reads and signs, but he is the one who willed it, inspired it and authorized it. Even more than in the statements he made at the Consistory, his authorship is evident from the continuity of the proposals contained in the text in conjunction with the orientation of his pontificate. In Part Two we shall document this continuity with various themes, but for the present we shall simply note the novelty of the proposed examination of conscience suggested in the memorandum.

The novelty consists in this: the memorandum passes beyond particular "confessions of sin" to a general confession that covers two thousand years. To be more precise, there is a transition from the individual acknowledgments of historical responsibility to a comprehensive examination of the history of the Church in the light of the Gospel in order to identify the deviations that are found there.

Up to that moment, in more than fifteen years of his pontificate, Pope John Paul had acknowledged at least forty instances of sins and errors. He had already spoken, directly or indirectly, about responsibility for the treatment of Galileo, the Jews and Muslims, Hus and Luther, the Indians; the injustices of the Inquisition, the Mafia, racism; religious integralism, schism and the papacy, wars and injustice, and the treatment of the Blacks. After the issuance of the memorandum, there would be papal pronouncements on the Crusades, dictatorships, women, religious wars, and Rwanda. In sixteen out of the twenty-one cases we have selected for Part Two of this volume, the Pope had already spoken about them and asked forgiveness. Consequently, anyone who knew about these instances could not have been surprised at the suggestion made by the Pope. It was simply the harvest of what he had sown through the years. But anyone who was ignorant of the extent of the guilt would consider the memorandum apocryphal and would take a stand in opposition to the Pope's proposal.

Post factum we would say that prior to that memorandum, Pope John Paul had spoken very much, almost too much, and yet not enough about the essentials. It was the memorandum that brought to completion the work

done up to that time and triggered the later developments.

The twenty-three pages of the memorandum are
entitled "Reflections on the Great Jubilee of the Year
Two Thousand" *(Riflessioni sul Grande Giubileo dell'Anno
Duemila)*. The principal initiatives suggested to the cardinals, who were asked for their opinion, were five in
number: the convocation of Synods for the Americas
and Asia; a meeting with all the Christian churches, and
another one with the Jews and Muslims; the updating of
the Martyrology; an attentive examination of the history
of the second millennium of the Church in order to "acknowledge the errors committed by its members and, in
a certain sense, in the name of the Church."

This last proposal is contained in paragraph 7 of
the memorandum and it bears the title, *Reconciliatio et
Paenitentia*: "As it approaches the end of the second millennium of Christianity, the Church should be aware
with ever greater clarity of how much the faithful have
proven to be unfaithful throughout the centuries, sin-
ning against Christ and his Gospel."

Recalling what had recently been done about the
Galileo case "to remedy the injustice inflicted on him,"
the Pope continues:

> A close look at the history of the second millennium
> can perhaps provide evidence of other similar errors,
> or even faults, as regards respect for the autonomy due
> the sciences. How can we be silent about so many kinds
> of violence perpetrated in the name of the faith? Reli-
> gious wars, courts of the Inquisition, and other viola-
> tions of the rights of the human person.... In the light
> of what Vatican Council II has said, the Church must
> on its own initiative examine the dark places of its his-
> tory and judge it in the light of Gospel principles.... It
> could be a grace of the coming Great Jubilee. It would

not in any way damage the moral prestige of the Church; on the contrary, it would be strengthened by the manifestation of loyalty and courage in admitting the errors committed by its members and, in a certain sense, in the name of the Church.

At the opening of the Consistory, the Pope verified that he was the author of the memorandum (something which had been doubted even publicly) and he repeated his suggestion for an examination of conscience at the end of the second millennium, against which there had already surfaced many objections both within and outside the Curia. Indirectly he also responded to those who were urging him to "give up the idea of an ecumenical meeting with Jews and Muslims on Mount Sinai as well as all self-criticism of the Catholic Church proposed in the memorandum to the cardinals."[25]

Hence, the Holy Father opened the Consistory with the words: "As I stated in the memorandum that I sent to each one of you." And shortly after that, he said: "In the cited memorandum I have stressed the opportunity for preparing a contemporary Martyrology." But even more important than the authorship of the memorandum is the restatement of the Pope's intention:

> With the approach of this Great Jubilee the Church needs a *metanoia,* that is, a discernment of the historical faults and failures of her members in responding to the demands of the Gospel. Only the courageous admission of the faults and omissions of which Christians are judged to be guilty to some degree, and also the generous intention to make amends, with God's help, can provide an efficacious initiative for the new evangelization and make the path to unity easier.

The Pope repeated his proposal energetically because it had aroused doubts and objections among the cardinals in a previous consultation conducted by mail. And there were doubts and objections expressed even during the work of the Consistory.

It seems that the majority of the cardinals had applauded the proposals for an ecumenical meeting of all the Christian churches, a series of Synods, and an updated Martyrology. At the same time, some amendments of the program were suggested: a Christological rather than an ecclesiological orientation would be preferable; the examination of conscience at the end of the second millennium should not overlook the present; it is necessary at all costs to avoid embarking on an interminable series of self-studies; care must be taken not to look at the past through the eyes of the present.

There was also a very significant difference on the basis of geographical origins. The cardinals from the East were fearful that an examination of conscience at the end of the second millennium could give rise to the anti-Catholic propaganda that was prevalent under the Communist regimes. The cardinals from the Third World showed a significant lack of interest in the historical quarrels of Europe, together with a fear that the admission of faults that are foreign to the culture of their people would have a negative impact and no particular pastoral advantages.

The preoccupation of the cardinals from former Communist countries was described by Cardinal Martini of Milan, who apparently did not attend the Consistory: "Among some there was some concern whether the suggestions of the Pope had been favorably received. Comments of this type came from cardinals from ex-Communist countries, where the Church has been subjected to a bombardment of accusations. It is not that they were looking for a reason for a total rejection, but historical factors played a big role."[26]

The Brazilian Cardinal Moreira Neves, OP, declared: "But no one intended to discourage the idea of a self-examination and renewal and no one excluded the possibility of reviewing some sad incidents of the past, similar to the Galileo case."[27]

Nevertheless, it is preferable perhaps to rely on the synthesis of the results of the previous consultations, presented at the opening of the Consistory by Cardinal Sodano, Secretary of State. However, since the only material from the Consistory that was published is the Pope's opening address, we have only second-hand reports concerning the debated material. Moreover, we have the impression that the points raised by Cardinal Sodano were later re-echoed in the *circuli minores.*

First of all, concerning the shift of emphasis from an ecclesiological to a Christological orientation, Cardinal Sodano reported: "There was general approval of the ecclesiological context of the historical survey, which was presented in a learned fashion. But at the same time, it seemed to some that it could possibly push the Christological aspect into the background...if there is too much emphasis on the ecclesiological problems, past and present."

Then there is the criticism of the examination of conscience:

> It is true that the Great Jubilee is also an occasion for the Church to reflect on the manner in which it has responded to the vocation which Christ has charged it to fulfill in the world.... But as regards a global, general examination of the past history of the Church, some of the cardinals have advised extreme caution and prudence, since this is a very difficult and delicate question, especially if it is handled in a summary fashion. Therefore, according to some, it would be preferable

for the Church's examination of conscience to consider, not the ages of antiquity which have already been studied in the context of their own time, but the present age which, in addition to its many bright spots, is not lacking shadows as well. The present age is our responsibility and therefore an examination of conscience is something that can be done and ought to be done.

In the end, the Secretary of State suggested that the entire question should be submitted to the judgment of the cardinals: "A public review of the dark periods in the history of the Church, in the light of the Gospel and the teaching of the Second Vatican Council, would have a special impact and importance. This could be done through the work of a few, but it should demonstrate in an especially credible and efficacious way the sincerity of adhesion to Christ on our part."

Strong support for the Pope was forthcoming from Cardinal Cassidy of Australia who, in a report immediately after the intervention by Cardinal Sodano, emphasized "the importance for the future" that would result from the purging of memories, if it is done with "an objective presentation of history, even when such objectivity would not be to the advantage of the ecclesial community." He asked that they admit that "we have not always been at the level that was expected of us in our relations with those who, in the majority of cases and without any fault on their part, did not share the riches that we enjoy."

It seems that a criticism of the Pope's memorandum was made by Cardinal Ratzinger concerning the ecclesiological orientation, which should be replaced by a Christological one. This had been stated in the previous consultation, but the Cardinal repeated it in the Consistory, more as a suggestion concerning procedure than as a criticism of the project as a whole. Cardinal Ruini made a similar intervention, while Cardinal Biffi of Bologna was decidedly in opposition.

In fact, Biffi is the only cardinal from whom we have detailed objections to the Pope's suggestion. He intervened in the Consistory, but again, we do not have a first-hand report of what he said. However, later on he wrote and spoke publicly on the question.

Cardinal Biffi, who was opposed, and Cardinal Etchegaray, who was favorable, are the only two cardinals who spoke openly on the subject. The other cardinals were generally shrouded in a kind of "cardinalatial reticence." The two cardinals were applauded, but I think that the applause was more justified for Biffi, who took the position of a critic. There is nothing more difficult for a cardinal than to criticize the pope. Since it is such a rarity, we shall quote at length from the commentary on self-criticism by the Church, contained in a book by Cardinal Biffi, published in 1995 under the title, *Christus Hodie* (Christ Today):

> *Self-Accusation and Repentance.* With great insistence Pope John Paul II exhorts us to prepare for the Great Jubilee of the year 2000 with a profound and sincere spirit of repentance and self-accusation. It is a topic of great importance and of great delicacy as well. It could become a source of ambiguity and even of spiritual uneasiness, especially among the young and the simple faithful, for whom the mysteries of the Kingdom (Mt 11:25) are primarily destined and to whom my solicitude as a pastor is primarily directed.
>
> *Repentance for Personal Sins.* The faults for which we should undoubtedly ask forgiveness from God and neighbor are those which each one of us commits by disobeying the Commandments and the all-embracing

precept of charity and by going against the judgments of a well-formed conscience. The call for individual conversion resounds from the very beginning of the preaching of Christ; it is always valid and relevant for all.

The Church Is Without Sin. Is the Church, precisely as Church, guilty of any sins? No; considered in the very truth of its being, the Church has no sins, because it is the "total Christ." He is the Head of the Church and the Son of God, to whom nothing morally objectionable can be imputed. But the Church can and ought to make its own the sentiments of sorrow and regret for the personal transgressions of its members.

Pope John Paul II expresses it this way: "Although she is holy because of her incorporation into Christ, the Church does not tire of doing penance: before God and man she always acknowledges as her own her sinful sons and daughters" (*Tertio Millennio Adveniente,* 33). Her children, not their sins, belong to the Church, although the sins of her children always deserve the tears of an undefiled mother.

With equal clarity the Encyclical Letter, *Ut Unum Sint,* states: "The Catholic Church acknowledges and confesses the weaknesses of her members, conscious that their sins are so many betrayals of and obstacles to the accomplishment of the Savior's plan. Because she feels herself constantly called to be renewed in the spirit of the Gospel, she does not cease to do penance. At the same time, she acknowledges and exalts still more the power of the Lord, who fills her with the gift of holiness, leads her forward, and conforms her to his Passion and Resurrection" (3).

This is the doctrine that I have received from St. Ambrose. For him, the wounds of sinful conduct are not inflicted on the Spouse of Christ, but on those who are the subjective agents. *Non in se sed in nobis Ecclesia vulneratur* (*De Virginitate,* 48). We are conjoined and belong to the "total Christ" insofar as we are holy, not insofar as we are not so. Our sinful actions are acts that in their essence are outside the Church *(extraecclesiali)*. Consequently, although made up of sinners, the Church is always holy: *Ex maculatis immaculata (In Lucam,* I, 17). Undoubtedly, in the eyes of the world the Church appears to be a sinner; but that is a fate that also befell the Spouse of the Church: *Merito speciem accipit peccatricis quia Christus quoque formam peccatoris accepit (Ibid.,* VI, 21).

Past Faults of the Church. Is it right and fitting that we should ask pardon for the errors of the Church in centuries past? Yes; it is right, because these have been proven by objective investigations, especially without any anachronistic estimates (something that doesn't always happen).

It can also serve to make us less defensive and improve our relationship with the representatives of the so-called lay culture. They would be pleased with our breadth of spirit, even if they will usually not find there any encouragement to overcome their state of incredulity.

But one should not neglect to emphasize that even when faults or errors have been committed by ecclesiastics having great responsibility, the Church has nevertheless continued to produce wonderful fruits of sanctity, thus demonstrating that it is always the Spouse of Christ, holy and immaculate. This emphasis seems to be especially necessary for the ordinary faithful who, since they do not know how to make theological distinctions, may find that their serene adhesion to the mystery of the Church has been shaken by these self-accusations.

An Unusual Act of Faith. It can be edifying, however, to note that the satisfaction that non-believers get in making accusations against the Church by the lies they have disseminated throughout their long history is an implicit act of faith in the Spouse of Christ, which continues to be present and active in every age of history with its identity unchanged. It is a remarkable continuity that has not been verified in any other social organism.

Some Examples. Galileo had been generally rejected in favor of the Ptolemaic theory in the universities of his day, and yet no rector or dean in our day has been called on to respond to the behavior of the academic authorities of those days. And who would dream of challenging the mayor of Milan or the president of the Lombard Region for the tragedies caused by the politics of Ludovico il Moro? And so it goes.

Anonymous Misdeeds. It goes without saying that the heinous historical crimes committed against the human race are hidden today under a mantle of silence. It seems that all are in agreement in saying that we are no longer responsible. For example, to whom will humanity send the bill for the countless French people sent to the guillotine in 1793, for no other crime than their social standing? To whom will humanity send the bill for the millions of Russian citizens slaughtered by the Bolsheviks? Therefore, as regards the sins of history, would it not be better for all of us to wait for the Last Judgment?[28]

Cardinal Biffi did not react negatively to the entire proposal of the Pope. There is nothing in his critique concerning the penitential, ecumenical and missionary aspects of the Pope's project. And these were key points in the proposal. For Cardinal Biffi, the element of repentance applies to individual persons, but Pope John Paul calls for a community dimension in the examination of conscience. The ecumenical aspect is not even mentioned in the critique by Cardinal Biffi, and the missionary element is implicitly contradicted when he says that the request for forgiveness will not help anyone to believe.

Cardinal Biffi treats exclusively of the risks involved in the initiative: the scandal to the simple faithful, the possible confusion about sin in the Church, the need to prove the errors by an objective investigation, the difficulty of avoiding anachronistic statements, and failure to accompany the admission of faults with the assertion that they have not prevented the Church from producing the fruits of sanctity.

Strictly speaking, Cardinal Biffi was simply advising prudence in the manner of conducting and concluding the examination proposed by the Pope. He does not say explicitly whether the examination of conscience should be made or not. But the tone of his critique is such that it would be better not to do it, although the Cardinal certainly would not publicly say as much. We shall now see how the Pope responded, or better yet, had to respond to Cardinal Biffi and the others who reacted negatively.[29]

NINE

Wojtyla Goes on Alone

The Pope did not convince all the cardinals, so he proceeded alone. He answered their objections by word and deed, or else he had others respond. He gave them his first general response in the Apostolic Letter, *Tertio Millennio Adveniente* (November 14, 1994). A more detailed reply was later issued by the papal theologian, Georges Cottier, OP, at the end of 1995. This Swiss Dominican is not only the "theologian for the pontifical household," but he also presides over the historico-theological commission, which is the most important commission for the Great Jubilee. It is in charge of the examination of conscience at the end of the second millennium. The text was published in 1996 without any fanfare, under the title, *La Chiesa Davanti alla Conversione: Il Frutto Più Significativo dell'Anno Santo* (The Church Faced with Conversion: The Most Important Fruit of the Holy Year). In the meantime the precise responses to the objections of the cardinals were released, and they can be placed under three headings:

— introduction of the program of the Great Jubilee, in continuity with the papal memorandum to the cardinals and the Apostolic Letter, *Tertio Millennio Adveniente*;

— coherent expansion of the ecumenical mea culpa;[30]

— the re-examination of history applied to the theme of women, formerly not treated.[31]

These conclusions and developments can be interpreted as responses to the cardinals in a twofold sense: they acknowledge the need for caution and prudence in language and procedure, but they reject the criticism that the project as a whole is inopportune.

Tertio Millennio Adveniente

To measure the effectiveness of the response to objections contained in the Apostolic Letter, it is helpful to recall the stages through which the Pope's proposal has passed, as described in the preceding Chapter:

— presented tentatively in the responses to the cardinals, it meets with cautious criticism and strong public objections that were scarcely noticed by the media, due to the lack of information about the text of the Pope's memorandum;

— Pope John Paul proposes it again at the Extraordinary Consistory and receives objections, both old and new;

— the Pope decides to proceed nevertheless and he confirms the decision with the Apostolic Letter on preparation for the Great Jubilee.

Here is the statement concerning the examination of conscience at the end of the millennium and the Pope's defense of it:

Hence it is appropriate that, as the second millennium of Christianity draws to a close, the Church should become more fully conscious of the sinfulness of her children, recalling all those times in history when they departed from the spirit of Christ and his Gospel and, instead of offering to the world the witness of a life inspired by the values of faith, indulged in ways of thinking and acting which were truly forms of counter-witness and scandal....

The Holy Door of the Jubilee of the Year 2000 should be symbolically wider than those of previous Jubilees, because humanity, upon reaching this goal, will leave behind not just a century but a millennium. It is fitting that the Church should make this passage with a clear awareness of what has happened to her during the last ten centuries. She cannot cross the threshold of the new millennium without encouraging her children to purify themselves, through repentance, of past errors and instances of infidelity, inconsistency, and slowness to act. Acknowledging the weaknesses of the past is an act of honesty and courage which helps us to strengthen our faith, which alerts us to face today's temptations and challenges, and prepares us to meet them (*Tertio Millennio Adveniente*, 33).

This defense of the Pope's proposal differs from the one indicated in the memorandum. The emphasis there was on the overall effect *ad extra* of the examination of conscience at the end of the millennium ("it will not in any way harm the moral prestige of the Church; rather, it will emerge strengthened"); but here it is the effect *ad intra* that is stressed, namely, a more complete conversion of the Church rather than an attempt to convince its opponents. One senses here the effect of the criticism by Cardinal Biffi and others, who saw very little apologetic value to the examination of conscience.

Georges Cottier

The article by the papal theologian, *La Chiesa Davanti alla Conversione* (September, 1996), is very important. At the time that it was written it was the most thorough interpretation and defense of the proposed self-examination. Upon reading it, one suspects that the Dominican theologian had been authorized by the Pope to answer the objections that had been raised. That is implied especially in the following statements:

— that the Church should admit the sins of its members but also (and this is something different) "their imperfections in their *imitatio Christi*" (their imitation of Christ), because it is a duty of the Church to ask itself continually about the "sins of its members" and "its own history" (a response to the objectors who had insisted that the Church is without sin);

— "the living memory of the Church is inseparable from the awareness of its identity throughout the centuries" and "the rereading of history in a spirit of repentance has great significance for the unity of the Church in time" (the response to those who compare the Church to other institutions, by suggesting that it is expedient to forego any judgment on the past);

— calling attention to the connection between "theological perspective" and "historical science" without imposing one over the other (the response to those who fear an anachronistic interpretation);

— "although good faith excuses, this does not mean that any behavior which we disapprove of today could have been objectively correct in its time" (a response to anyone who says, for example, that the

Crusades were justified because the men who took part in them were in good faith);

— "the awareness of attending circumstances does not excuse the Church from repentance" (the answer to those who would explain everything by historical circumstances).

Toward the Great Jubilee

Beginning in 1996, the program for the Great Jubilee was distributed to all the principal sectors of the Church. It is a grandiose project, perhaps even exaggerated, and it will engage the offices and energies of the Church through the year 2000.

The first international meeting of the Central Committee for the Great Jubilee was held at the Vatican on February 15 and 16, 1996, consisting of representatives from the local churches. There were 107 delegates from the national conferences of bishops and the churches of the Eastern rite. In addition, there were six delegates from the sister churches: the Patriarchate of Constantinople, the Anglican Church, the World Federation of Lutherans, the Worldwide Alliance of Reformed Churches, the World Council of the Methodist Church, and the CEC.

The impression carried away by the participants was that the program for the Great Jubilee is moving along coherently, thanks to the initial input from Pope John Paul II. Perhaps the early outline was considered somewhat excessive, but the finalized program embodies all the essential points of the Jubilee as envisioned by Pope John Paul: ecumenical, interreligious, historical and social. At the moment one could say that nothing that was truly original and creative has been lost. Consequently, it is possible to trace a cohesive development of the various phases up until the present time:

— from the Pope's memorandum to the cardinals at the beginning of 1994 to the discussions in the Extraordinary Consistory on June 13 and 14, 1994;

— from the Apostolic Letter, *Tertio Millennio Adveniente* (November 14, 1994) to the formation of the Central Committee (March 16, 1995);

— from the publication of the first collegial work under the auspices of the Council of the President (the volume containing the essay by Georges Cottier, OP, December 15, 1995) to the first consultative meeting with the episcopate (February 15 and 16, 1996).

Before passing on to a detailed examination of the composition and work of the historico-theological commission, we shall glance at the references to a re-examination of history and the examination of conscience that can be found in the work of the other commissions. It is clear from the available material that the examination of conscience at the end of the millennium is not just one program among others; it is, as the Pope intended and as interpreted by Cardinal Etchegaray and others, the key to the discussion of all the themes of the complex program. There is a total of eight commissions, and at least four of them have shown great interest in the examination of conscience, which was entrusted to the historico-theological commission. In addition to this, the notion of an examination of conscience made a strong impression on the ecumenical commission, as well as on the commissions dealing with interreligious dialogue and social questions.

At the present, in addition to Cardinal Etchegaray, President of the Committee, and Cardinal Sebastiani, Secretary, there are four other key members: Cardinal Arinze and Cardinal Cassidy (members of the Council of the president), Bishop Fortino (vice-president of the ecumenical commission), and Father Georges Cottier (president of the historico-theological commission).

First of all, the ecumenical commission, under the presidency of Bishop Paul Werner Scheele of Würzburg, is composed of ten Catholic members, together with six representatives of other churches and ecclesial communities as "adjunct members." That will allow for a more attentive examination of concrete ecumenical possibilities and it will also foster cooperation among the churches. This commission was at first listed in the directory of the central committee as having a predominant role, in view of the ecumenical dimension which the Holy Father wants to imprint on the close of the second millennium.

The purpose of the commission is to find ways for ecumenical cooperation, first in the preparation and then in the celebration of the year 2000. This is done in the hope that during that year it will be possible to organize a pan-Christian meeting so that all Christians can publicly and solemnly profess their common faith. Then (and this is the re-examination of history that is of interest to us) there will be a reflection on the Jubilees of the past that have caused strong tensions with other Christians, bearing in mind that the celebration of a Jubilee Year is a Catholic practice unknown to the Orthodox and opposed by the Reformation and the heirs of the Reformation.

The commission for interreligious dialogue, under the presidency of Archbishop Michael L. Fitzgerald, does not want to present the Jubilee Year as an exclusively Christian event, with no concern for other religions and much less for those opposed to religion. Like the ecumenical commission, its task is to prepare a prayer meeting with Jews, Muslims and representatives of other religions, to whom it will present the Jubilee Year as an occasion for a reciprocal examination of conscience, a moment of repentance and forgiveness.

The social commission, headed by Father Diarmuid Martin, secretary of the Council for Justice and Peace, will also provide an opportunity to work for the re-examination of history. It will suggest initiatives for making the year 1999 a true year of charity, ranging from personal conversion to fulfillment of international obligations. Moreover, that the year 2000 may be a year of peace, "actions will be taken on a large scale to promote the cessation of hostilities among peoples by a laying down of arms and by having recourse also to symbolic gestures, prayer vigils and fasting."

Historico-Theological Commission

The president of this commission is the Swiss Dominican, Father Georges Cottier, theologian of the papal household. The vice-president is the Jesuit, Father Rino Fisichella, professor of fundamental theology at the Gregorian University. The commission is divided into two sections; Father Cottier is in charge of the historical section, and Father Fisichella, the theological section.[32]

The historical section will bring to light the dark pages of the history of the Church, so that a spirit of *metanoia* will lead to the request for forgiveness. For the moment, the commission is delaying the study of particular cases of authors and famous personages (for example, Savonarola, Hus, Las Casas) in order to look again at two historical themes that have ecclesial, his-

torical and cultural significance, namely, anti-Semitism
and the Inquisition. This re-evaluation of history will
probably call for two international congresses of great
scientific value, to be held in Rome before the celebration of the Great Jubilee.

Cardinal Sebastiani supported this project at the
meeting of the Council in 1996: "The commission is
convinced that this choice will assure an understanding
of the events that actually took place; will help in the
discovery of historical truth, without being influenced
by subjective polemics; and could serve as a basis for the
creation of a new culture that is not founded on any
kind of prejudice. At the same time it will make it possible to fulfill the desire of the Holy Father to perform
concrete acts of forgiveness."

The desire of the Holy Father! As regards the topics
selected, it would seem that in the Catholic system only
the Pope can say, "We made a mistake." And that seems
to be the case even after the Pope has said to proceed
with the re-examination of history. Everything must be
referred to him.

At that same meeting in 1996, Cardinal Etchegaray
and Father Georges Cottier confirmed that the material
is subject entirely to the Pope's decision and it would
have to be developed along those lines. Father Cottier
expressed it this way: "The historical problem is being
studied because the Holy Father has inserted it in *Tertio
Millennio Adveniente*. Whatever pertains to particular
cases or personalities will be handled by the congresses,
in which, with the help of historians, an attempt will be
made to discover the historical truth. After that will
come the judgment as to the expediency and the
method of admitting mistakes. In any case, this aspect
of the Jubilee should be looked upon as positive, joyful
and not negative."

There were some persons at the 1996 meeting, specifically invited by the Pope or sent by the bishops' conferences, who voiced objections. Some of these were a repetition of objections raised at the Extraordinary Consistory in 1994: we are looking only at the past, with a "reductive" mentality; there is no evident connection between historical problems and the Great Jubilee; there are also positive aspects in the history of the Church; a discussion of the Inquisition could revive the old atheistic propaganda in former Communist countries. Responding to these fears, Cardinal Etchegaray assured the objectors that the historico-theological commission is well aware of the importance and delicacy of these questions. They will present proposals for evaluation and decision by the presidential council. However, in all things they will follow the directions given by the Holy Father in *Tertio Millennio Adveniente*.

Hence, the course is clearly charted. Father Cottier will oversee the work; Cardinal Etchegaray will be his Vatican overseer; the Holy Father will be the ultimate judge. The work will be done, say Cottier and Etchegaray, and it will be ample and well articulated so that it can be given proper emphasis, without any undue force, lights and shadows. The structure of a Congress is ideal for airing various opinions, but it will be up to the Pope to decide how to proceed to the admission of errors. We already have the experience of dealing with the Galileo case; it will suffice to follow along the same lines. However, at that time no Congress was held. Rather a commission was appointed to coordinate the findings of the four sub-commissions. Then, after ten years of work, a report was finally compiled by the president and an emissary of the Pope. It is logical to presume that the two Congresses scheduled in preparation for the Great Jubilee will be able to compile a similar report, followed by papal verification.

It is up to the Commission to study the ways of examining how the People of God have accepted the objectives of this project and the reforms of the Second Vatican Council. At the same time, the Commission will further develop the theme of repentance and, together with this, take up the question of indulgences. This thorny question of indulgences also calls for a re-examination of history, for this is what ignited the spark of the Lutheran Reformation.

But even more interesting, although much less provocative, is the study of the reception of the changes brought about by the last Council. As Cardinal Sebastiani pointed out in the meeting we have mentioned, there are four questions that have to be confronted, as indicated by Pope John Paul II: how "the primacy of the Word of God" was received, as mentioned in the document *Dei Verbum*; the ecclesiology of *communio*, as taught in *Lumen Gentium*; the statement on the liturgy in *Sacrosanctum Concilium*; and the dialogue between the Church and the world as described in *Gaudium et Spes*. Nothing has been overlooked. Cardinal Sebastiani concluded: "The analysis of these great themes will be made in the light of the extraordinary Synod of 1985, which marked the twentieth anniversary of the Second Vatican Council." The 1985 revision was a stimulus, and not a roadblock in spite of the fears of the watchmen. It is to be expected that the same thing will happen in the examination of conscience at the end of the millennium.

Anti-Semitism and the Inquisitions

What will be the result of the two international Congresses which are scheduled to take place in Rome for discussing these two topics? There were no reliable indications when we completed our investigation. But as regards anti-Semitism, it is possible to be a bit more precise regarding the expectation to which the scheduled Congress could respond. As to the Inquisitions, we know why it was decided to put this word in the plural and with the help of an accredited historian we can specify the nub of the question.

As regards anti-Semitism, the coming international Congress could activate the project mentioned in the Vatican document on the Holocaust ten years ago. It was spoken of many times but nothing ever came of it. The first attempt goes back to a meeting held to clarify the situation when the Jews protested against the papal audience granted to Waldheim on June 25, 1987. The meeting took place two months later, on August 31 and September 1, between representatives from the Holy See and a delegation from the International Jewish Commission for Interreligious Consultation. At the conclusion of the meeting, Cardinal Willebrands, who headed the Vatican delegation, announced that the commission for religious contacts with Judaism intended to prepare an official Catholic statement on the Holocaust, on the historical premises of anti-Semitism, and its manifestations in modern times.

A forecast of the possible content of such a document was projected in the *Dichiarazione di Praga* (the Prague Declaration) published on September 6, 1990, by the international committee for Catholic-Jewish relations: "Some traditional Catholic thought, teaching, preaching, and practice during the patristic and medieval periods have contributed to the rise of anti-Semitism in Western society. In modern times many Catholics have not been sufficiently vigilant in reacting against anti-Semitic demonstrations. The Catholic delegates have condemned both anti-Semitism and all forms of racism as sins against God and against humanity. One cannot be authentically Christian and at the same time practice anti-Semitism."

The coming Congress could make a contribution to the document on the Holocaust and this document could be at the same time an occasion for asking forgiveness from the Jews, which was often suggested but never carried out.

As to the Inquisitions, Father Georges Cottier, president of the Commission, has already explained at a meeting with representatives of the bishops' conferences (February 15-16, 1996), why the word is in the plural. "It is more correct," he said, "to speak of Inquisitions because we are dealing with an historical phenomenon that is defined differently from place to place."

What is likely to be the conclusion of the Congress? It could result in a definitive document of admission of injustices of the kind referred to by Cardinal Poupard in the Galileo case. These injustices, or others similar to them, could be the subject of such a document:

> The acceptance of denunciations and the safeguarding of the secrecy of the accusers; the usual exclusion of a defender; the excessive widening of the definition of heresy; the use of torture, even within the limits and restrictions of the law; and the death penalty are all acts contrary to the genuine spirit of the Gospel. It must be admitted that at least in these areas the modern age, even with its errors and deviations, has better understood the exigencies of the Christian message.[33]

PART TWO

Pronouncements by John Paul II

ONE

The Crusades

S ince June 14, 1996, the Piazza delle Crociate (The Piazza of the Crusades) in Milan is called Piazza Paolo VI (Piazza of Paul VI). In Rome, what was formerly called the via del Sant'Uffizio (way of the Holy Office [Inquisition]) is now named via Paolo VI (way of Paul VI). As is fitting, it is Montini whose name signals the change, but it is Wojtyla who more frequently has made revisions in one or another chapter in the history of the Church. And such is the case with the Crusades. This is the way Pope John Paul II spoke on February 12, 1995, when he referred to St. Catherine of Siena in his Sunday meditation prior to reciting the Angelus:

> The cry with which Catherine turned to Pope Gregory XI to encourage him to be a herald of peace among Christians is well known: "Peace, peace, peace, my sweet father, and no more war!" (Letter 218).... Of course, we must recognize that she was also a daughter of her time, when, justly eager to defend the holy places, she adopted the then prevailing mentality that this task could be accomplished even by recourse to fighting. Today we ought to be grateful to the Spirit of God, who has enabled us to understand ever more clearly that the appropriate way to deal with problems that can arise

between peoples, religions and cultures, one which is also most in harmony with the Gospel, is that of patient, firm and respectful dialogue. Nevertheless, Catherine's zeal remains an example of brave, strong love, an encouragement to devote our efforts to all possible strategies of constructive dialogue in order to build an increasingly stable and far-reaching peace (*L'Osservatore Romano* [English edition], February 15, 1995).

These are solemn words that do not apply directly and precisely to the Crusades, which were also a Christian undertaking, but they do demonstrate a complete change of perspective in the name of the Gospel. The change of attitude is even more striking if one takes into account the fact that it was the popes themselves who launched the Crusades, and then tried for centuries to make the Christian princes assume the obligation of carrying them on.

One thing that Pope John Paul did not say (and it is understandable, because one pope never criticizes another; perhaps he may contradict him in action but never with words) is that Catherine gave her support to the Crusades in obedience to Gregory XI and to the General Chapter of the Dominican Order, to which she belonged. In the years between 1376 and 1380 Catherine always insisted that three distinct goods could come from the Crusades: peace for Christians, penance for the soldiers, and salvation for many Muslims (meaning that if taken prisoner, they would be forced to be baptized!). And what will happen to a Christian virgin who spends all her energy in being obedient to the command of the pope? Six centuries later, another pope will hail her as "a daughter of her times"!

The topic of the Crusades can be linked to that of Islam and to the topics of war and peace and the religious wars. Pope John Paul may have felt some hesitation in referring explicitly to the Crusades thus running the risk of applying retroactively to the Second Vatican Council a judgment on the medieval period. After all, the leaders and intellectuals of the Islamic world continue to blame the popes for the "armed pilgrimages" (as the historian Cardini wants us to call the Crusades) which soon became military expeditions of conquest. The Crusades were recalled by the Muslim leaders when they refused to meet with Pope John Paul II in Nigeria in February, 1982, and in Kenya in September, 1995. Moreover, the African Synod convoked by the Pope and held in Rome in 1994 was branded by conservative Muslims from Arabian countries as a "Crusade against Islam."

But can a Muslim understand a pope who distances himself from the Crusades? The response is affirmative. That is how the Muslim intellectual, Khaled Fouad Allam, who participated in the interreligious meeting at Assisi in 1986, commented on Pope John Paul's omission of any reference to the Crusades: "The invitation of the Pope to a 'patient, firm but respectful' dialogue among religions is objectively a change of perspective regarding the Crusades. His is a perspective which I, a non-Christian, judge to be genuinely evangelical."[34]

And can the Christian world understand self-criticism by the Pope? I am not referring to the experts and scholars, but to pastors and catechists. Here also the response is affirmative, as long as one does not pay too much attention to the specific purpose of the Crusades, but to the more general problem of relations between the Muslim and Christian worlds. Actually, the question of the Crusades is a small and academic problem if we place it against the much larger question of the relationship between Muslims and Christians. Therefore, if we frame the question correctly, it is enormous, and not at all a distant and purely historical one. Today also there are tensions between Islam and the Christian (or post-Christian) world which seem to be tending toward a resolution by means of force and violence.

This is how the *Catechismo degli Adulti* (Catechism for Adults), published by the Italian Conference of Bishops, speaks of the Crusades in the context of the difficulty of dialogue with Islam: "The memory of the past still weighs heavily. Ten centuries of violent opposition have seen repeated attempts on the part of Arabs and Turks to invade Europe and on the part of the West, the Crusades during the medieval period and forced colonization in modern times. Today the secularized, individualistic and consumer-oriented culture of the West is penetrating the Islamic world and corroding it from within, thus provoking the reaction of Muslim fundamentalism, which also involves an aversion to Christianity." This judgment on the Crusades is the same as that of the Pope and corresponds to his concern that Islam no longer look at the Christian world as an armed coalition on the move to thrust it back.

TWO

Dictatorships

This chapter is yet to be written and it pertains more to the national Catholic communities than to the popes. John Paul II gets the credit for having included this title in the self-examination, thus involving the bishops of the local churches in the process, and having indicated, in reference to Nazi Germany, the essential question to which all must respond. Under this title of dictatorships the Pope invites them, in view of the coming of a new millennium, to examine themselves concerning the acquiescence of the faithful in confronting totalitarian regimes. As we shall see, the Pope speaks of "not a few Christians," but he really meant to say "many" or even "too many" Christians have passively accepted such regimes. And he was not speaking only of the past; he said "in our day." So the precise purpose of the examination of conscience on this point is: To what extent did the Christian community oppose the violations of basic human rights in this or that totalitarian regime? The indication given by the Pope at Berlin in 1996 was that it was "all too little" that the Catholic Church did against the Nazi regime. However, the inclusion of this topic in the self-examination

was previously indicated by the Pope in this passage
from a document issued in 1994, referring to the preparation for the Great Jubilee:

> And with respect to the Church of our time, how can we
> not lament the lack of discernment, which at times be-
> came even acquiescence, shown by many Christians
> concerning the violation of fundamental human rights
> by totalitarian regimes? (*Tertio Millennio Adveniente,* 36).

The Pope distinguishes between the lack of discernment and acquiescence, indicating the sinfulness of the
first form of yielding, which does not imply acceptance
and adhesion, but does apply to some forms of neutral-
ity. One thinks also of the need to examine the behavior
of the Italian Catholic community during the Fascist
regime, and to investigate how much anti-Christian sentiment permeated Fascism after its alliance with Hitler
and the subsequent promulgation of laws on racial
purity. It is no small challenge which the Catholic
communities have received from this Polish Pope, who
personally experienced the Nazi occupation and the
Communist regime.

Wojtyla is not pointing the finger at totalitarian regimes as such, but on the violations of basic human
rights by those regimes. It is the same criterion that was
used by the Second Vatican Council in the document
Gaudium et Spes (1965) and it is the argument that has
enabled John Paul II to speak out against all dictatorial
systems in the course of his travels to Poland, Brazil, the
Philippines, Guatemala, Haiti, Chile, Paraguay and the
Sudan. He never referred directly and explicitly to any
form of government, but to the fundamental rights that
all forms of government should respect and protect.

The Polish experience and the direct contact with
Catholic communities in conflict with totalitarian re–

gimes, made possible by his travels, are at the root of this papal solicitude in view of the Great Jubilee. And it is no small gain for a century to end with a pope who raises the question of dictatorships, having spent more than half of its course with pontiffs, Curias, and Catholic communities that usually preferred authoritarian regimes (as long as they were favorable or tolerant toward the Church) over democratic ones.

But how should a Catholic community oppose a regime that violates human rights? The Pope does not give any specific indications in his Apostolic Letter, but on another occasion he stated publicly that the German Catholic Church did too little in opposing the Nazi regime. He made this terse statement, and it is all the more significant coming from the mouth of a Pole who is speaking German (Berlin, 1996), at a meeting with the central commission of Jews. Just previously he had beatified the priest, Bernhard Lichtenberg, who opposed the inhuman ideology of Nationalist Socialism and sacrificed his life for the faith:

> Even if, as recent history has demonstrated, many priests and many laypersons opposed that regime of terror and even if they used many kinds of opposition in their daily life, that was still too little (Berlin, June 23, 1996).

There were, according to the Pope, many individuals who protested publicly in defense of the Jews, and he mentioned Bernhard Lichtenberg, Margarete Sommer, Cardinal Konrad von Preysing, Maria Terwiel. There were also, as he said, anonymous acts of resistance in daily life. So what was lacking? The Pope did not say, but from the context one can conclude that what was missing was an official stand in the name of the entire Catholic Church in Germany.

The papal self-criticism was facilitated by a dramatic document issued by the German Conference of Bishops and published a year earlier, in January, 1995. It was written to mark the fiftieth anniversary of the liberation of prisoners from the concentration camp at Auschwitz. In the document the bishops admitted "the faults and defects" of Catholics, recalling that "not a few of them let themselves be taken in by the ideology of National Socialism and remained indifferent to the crimes against the life and property of the Jews. Some of them took part in the criminal acts and thus became criminals themselves."

But many years before that, the German bishops had made an explicit suggestion for papal self-examination in a declaration issued by the secretariat of the episcopacy in 1979. It contained a detailed summary of what bishops and the Catholic faithful did or did not do in opposing Nazism. The declaration then concludes that during the periods of most intensive persecution of the Jews (1933, 1935 and 1939), the Church did not take a sufficiently clear and firm stand against the violations of human rights.

Is it reasonable to suggest the possibility that the invitation of the Pope to rethink the relationships between the Church and dictatorships was heeded by those Catholic communities that have less reason to exercise this self-examination? We have an indication of the answer in the fact that the Pope's invitation has resulted in a document published by the bishops of Argentina on April 27, 1996:

> In the course of our national history, very often and in many ways the proclamation of the Gospel and its projection into political life have been completely separated from each other. The separation was manifested

in a cruel manner during the 60's and 70's, a period marked by the terrorism of guerilla warfare and repressive tactics by the State. The deep wounds that have been inflicted are still not healed.

Without admitting a responsibility that the Church did not have for those deeds, we must nevertheless admit that there were Catholics who defended and participated in systematic violence as a form of "national liberation," trying to overthrow the political authority and set up a new type of society inspired by Marxist ideology, which unfortunately attracted many young people. And there were not lacking other groups, among whom there were numerous sons of the Church, who took part illegally in guerilla warfare in an immoral and heinous manner, which is a cause for shame for all of us. For that reason it is time for us to confirm what we have already said: if any members of the Church, whatever their condition, have cooperated by their membership or their complicity in those acts, they have done so with personal responsibility against God, against humanity and against their own conscience....

In solidarity with our people and the sins of all, we implore pardon from the Lord our God for the crimes committed, and especially for those in which the protagonists were sons of the Church, whether in the ranks of revolutionary guerilla warfare or among those who held power in the State or were members of the security forces, and also for those who, distorting the teaching of Christ, instigated others to engage in the violence of guerilla warfare or unjust repression.

At that moment the episcopate felt obliged to find a way to voice, on the one hand, its strong denunciation of all acts of violence and, on the other hand, the frequent acts of repression by the political authorities; whether the latter would be done by those of the executive council of the Bishops' Conference of Argentina, or the commission of bishops in charge of such matters, or by the actions of individual bishops. They were all trying to find practical solutions so that the persons detained would not have to undergo even greater suffering. We must confess that unfortunately we came up against the intransigence of many authorities; they rose up as an impenetrable wall. Some people maintained that at that moment the bishops should have broken off all contacts with the authorities, thinking that such a rupture would have been an effective means for obtaining the release of the detained persons. Only God knows what would have happened if we had gone in that direction. But there is no doubt that all that was done was not enough to put an end to such an atrocity....

We regret deeply that we were not able to do more to lessen the suffering caused during that traumatic period. We are in solidarity with those who feel injured and we regret sincerely the participation of sons of the Church in the violation of human rights.

Before approving the text, the bishops of Argentina discussed the draft of another, more forthright, text that much more resembled the style of Pope John Paul. It contained a more explicit admission of guilt, but it did not receive the required majority of votes:

Now, at some distance from those years and in the light of the letter of John Paul II concerning the Great Jubilee, after reviewing our pastoral action during the grave and painful emergency in our recent past, we bishops admit that we were not able to discern clearly the events that we were interpreting. We were unable to understand or evaluate the gravity of the evil that was afflicting the social body, especially the abuses committed against the dignity of persons called before those who should have guaranteed them due legal process. In virtue of the responsibility that is ours, for all that we have neglected to do or about which we have remained

silent; for all that we were unable to do because of inde-
cision, weakness or an erroneous judgment of events;
for all that we have failed to do at the proper time; for
all that we did in a lukewarm or unworthy manner; for
all that, we ask God's forgiveness from the bottom of
our hearts.[35]

THREE

Division among the Churches

I n this chapter we are at the heart of the examination of conscience proposed by Pope John Paul II for the end of the millennium. The first fault to be confessed is that of division. The confession must be complete and its expression exemplary. This topic, division among the churches, is also related to the chapters on the religious wars, Luther, and the schism of the East, in each of which we shall report on specific statements. Here, however, we treat the subject of division in general and offer some comments on methodology.

There are three basic sources for our discussion: (1) the memorandum sent to the cardinals for the Extraordinary Consistory in the springtime of 1994; (2) the Apostolic Letter, *Tertio Millennio Adveniente,* promulgated in November of the same year; (3) the Encyclical, *Ut Unum Sint,* issued in May, 1995.

These three texts constitute a unified corpus and they mark the mature stage of the pontificate of John Paul II. Chronologically these three documents were preceded by three separate suggestions made by the Pope at ecumenical meetings in 1980 and 1983, at Paris, Mainz and Vienna, and by two more direct and specific references at the opening and closing of the European Synod in 1991.

A scanning of the texts reveals that from the very beginning, Pope John Paul had the idea that reciprocal forgiveness was the preferred way for the ecumenical movement to follow. Perhaps his conviction stemmed in great part from the documents of the Second Vatican Council and the teaching of Pope Paul VI. The idea was personalized and made more specific by the grand ecumenical dream toward which his pontificate was moving by the end of the 1980's. Finally, it became a dominant concept in the preparations for the Great Jubilee at the end of the second millennium. It is also very likely to become the most lasting heritage of the pontificate of Pope Wojtyla.

Purification of the Memory

With the passing years, the concept of a "purification of the memory" has become a fundamental password in the pontificate of John Paul II. Its first formulation was stated in reference to the struggles among Christians:

> First and foremost, and in the dynamics of the movement toward unity, our personal and community memory must be purified of the memory of all the conflicts, injustice and hatred of the past. This purification is carried out through mutual forgiveness, from the depths of our hearts, which is the condition of the blossoming of real brotherly charity, a charity that is not resentful and that excuses everything (cf. 1 Cor 13:5 and 7).... You are facing this task and I rejoice particularly at the quality of the collaboration that exists among you, especially as regards the service of man, a service understood in its whole dimension and which

requires urgently and immediately the testimony of all Christians, the necessity of which I have already stressed in the Encyclical *Redemptor Hominis* (Meeting with the leaders of other Christian communities, Paris, May 31, 1980).

Confession of Faults

The purification of memory can become a reality with the confession of faults:

Our being together in your German homeland confronts us with the event of the Reformation. We must think of what preceded it and of what has happened since. If we do not evade the facts, we realize that the faults of men led to the unhappy division of Christians, and that our faults again hinder the possible and necessary steps toward unity. I emphatically make my own what my predecessor Adrian VI said in 1523 at the Diet of Nuremberg: "Certainly the Lord's hand has not been shortened so much that he cannot save us, but sin separates us from him.... All of us, prelates and priests, have strayed from the right path and there is not anyone who does good (cf. Ps 14:3). Therefore we must all render honor to God and humble ourselves before him. Each of us must consider why he has fallen and judge himself rather than be judged by God on the day of wrath." With the last German or Dutch pope I say: "The disease is deep-rooted and developed: we must therefore proceed step by step, and first of all treat the most serious and dangerous ills with suitable medicines, so as not to make things even more confused with a hasty reform." Today, as then, the first and most important step toward unity is the renewal of Christian life. "There can be no ecumenism worthy of the name without interior conversion" (*Unitatis Redintegratio,* 7; Meeting with representatives of other Christian Churches, Mainz, November 17, 1980).

We shall again meet Pope Adrian VI when we speak about Luther, but already in Part One we saw some references to the non-Italian pope of the Renaissance by the first non-Italian pope in modern times. And here is another synthetic expression of the same self-accusing attitude which has become symptomatic of his pontificate: "The grave guilt with which Christians have burdened themselves cannot, must not, be denied" (Ecumenical meeting, Vienna, September 11, 1983).

Always Forgive

Only forgiveness can really purify the historical memory of the faults that have been acknowledged.

> At the close of this dramatic century, Peter's question seems to take on a special importance: "Lord, how often must I forgive?" (Mt 18:21).
>
> The answer that Christ gives in the parable is also expressed in the Sermon on the Mount: "Blessed are the merciful, for they will be shown mercy" (Mt 5:7). In fact, we should always forgive, remembering that we too are in need of forgiveness. We need to be forgiven much more often than we need to forgive (Opening of the Synod of Europe, St. Peter's, November 28, 1991).
>
> The saving message of which we are heralds, will be accepted by the people of our time only if it is accompanied by a consistent witness. The Second Vatican Council states that "there can be no ecumenism worthy of the name without a change of heart. For it is from the renewal of our minds, from self-denial and an unstinted love that desires of unity take their rise and develop" (*Unitatis Redintegratio,* 7). In the light of that principle, it is fitting that we should examine ourselves concerning the direction which dialogue must take in accordance with the demands of the Gospel.
>
> These are the demands of truth and of love. They presuppose a frank recognition of the facts, together

with a readiness to forgive and to make amends for our respective mistakes. They prevent us from shutting ourselves up within preconceptions, so often a source of bitterness and fruitless recriminations. They prevent us from making groundless accusations against our brother, imputing to him intentions and aims which he does not have. Thus, when we are impelled by a desire to understand fully the other's position, disagreements are settled through patient and sincere dialogue, under the guidance of the Holy Spirit, the Paraclete (Ecumenical celebration at the close of the Synod of Europe, St. Peter's, December 7, 1991).

The full significance of these two calls for forgiveness among Christians lies in the fact that they were spoken at the opening and closing of the Synod of Europe (1991), which marked a very difficult moment in the relations between the Catholic and the Orthodox Churches. The mutual dialogue referred to in the second quote had a decisive precedent in yet another meeting which was also presided over by the Pope on December 5, 1985. It took place at the conclusion of the Extraordinary Synod which marked the twentieth anniversary of the close of the Second Vatican Council. It also served as a summation of the numerous ecumenical meetings that had taken place during the travels of Pope John Paul. After the homily there was a gesture of reconciliation and the kiss of peace, described as follows by the Jesuit commentator, Giovanni Caprile, the principal reporter on the Second Vatican Council and various synods: "The celebrant invited all those present to admit their own sins, especially those which have provoked and kept alive the separation of Christians. A lector addressed three petitions to the Lord Jesus: that he intervene to reconcile us to one another, to heal our wounds and the sins of division, and to lead us into eternal life. The celebrant concluded by imploring forgiveness and help in being sincere in pardoning each other. Then followed the kiss of peace, beginning with the Pope and the non-Catholic brethren."

The Mea Culpa as an Ecumenical Gesture

With the memorandum sent by the Pope to the cardinals in the spring of 1994, the examination of Catholic responsibility for the division of the churches became a task that was proposed to all:

> With an attitude of full receptivity to the action of the Holy Spirit, the Church and Christians fulfill this task with renewed diligence in approaching the year 2000. The immanence of the end of the second millennium invites all to an examination of conscience and to suitable ecumenical initiatives, so that in the face of the Great Jubilee they may find themselves, if not fully reconciled, at least in less opposition and division than they were during the course of this second millennium (Memorandum sent to the cardinals in the spring of 1994).[36]

The Greatest Duty

At the opening of the Extraordinary Consistory in 1994, the Holy Father repeated his request for a mea culpa, as he had suggested previously in his memorandum to the cardinals. It had provoked a great reaction in the public opinion as well as some criticism from within the Church, as we have already indicated in Chapter 8 of Part One. Here, then, is what the Pope said:

> In view of the year 2000, this is perhaps the greatest task. We cannot come before Christ, the Lord of his-

tory, as divided as we have unfortunately been during the second millennium. These divisions must give way to rapprochement and harmony; the wounds on the path of Christian unity must be healed. As she faces this Great Jubilee, the Church needs a *"metanoia,"* that is, a discernment of her children's historical short-comings and negligence with regard to the demands of the Gospel. Only the courageous acknowledgment of faults and omissions, for which Christians have in some way been responsible, as well as the generous intention to remedy them with the help of God, can give an effective impetus to the new evangelization and make the path to unity easier (Extraordinary Consistory, St. Peter's, June 13, 1994).

The First Sin

At the conclusion of this introductory phase for the mea culpa, the Pope indicated in his letter on the Great Jubilee that the first sin that must be amended is that of the division of the churches:

> Among the sins which require a greater commitment to repentance and conversion should certainly be counted those which have been detrimental to the unity willed by God for his People. In the course of the thousand years now drawing to a close, even more than in the first millennium, ecclesial communion has been painfully wounded, a fact "for which, at times, men of both sides were to blame" (*Unitatis Redintegratio,* 3). Such wounds openly contradict the will of Christ and are a cause of scandal to the world. These sins of the past unfortunately still burden us and remain ever present temptations. It is necessary to make amends for them, and earnestly to beseech Christ's forgiveness (*Tertio Millennio Adveniente,* 34).

All Must Make Amends

In his Encyclical, *Ut Unum Sint,* Pope John Paul proceeds from the duty to make amends for the sins on both sides to a call for mutual forgiveness:

> All the sins of the world were gathered up in the saving sacrifice of Christ, including the sins committed against the Church's unity: the sins of Christians, those of the pastors no less than those of the lay faithful. Even after the many sins which have contributed to our historical divisions, Christian unity is possible, provided that we are humbly conscious of having sinned against unity and are convinced of our need for conversion. Not only personal sins must be forgiven and left behind, but also social sins, which is to say the sinful "structures" themselves which have contributed and can still contribute to division and to the reinforcing of division.... The Catholic Church must enter into what might be called a "dialogue of conversion," which constitutes the spiritual foundation of ecumenical dialogue. In this dialogue, which takes place before God, each individual must recognize his own faults, confess his sins and place himself in the hands of the One who is our Intercessor before the Father, Jesus Christ (*Ut Unum Sint,* 34; 82).

The felicitous synthetic phrase, "dialogue of conversion" should be noted, as well as the bold reference to "social sins" and "structures" of sin. It is also noteworthy that the application of that terminology, which was further developed in the Synod of 1993, to the very life of the Church is without precedent. It follows on the heels of the assertion during the Consistory that the Church is without sin. And here is another response to the Consistory, in which the last paragraph on the purgation of the Church is especially important:

In the face of the divisions which have afflicted the Church down the centuries, it is impossible to be passive. Catholics and non-Catholics cannot but suffer acutely when they see their separations, in such contrast with Christ's heartfelt words at the Last Supper (cf. Jn 17:20-23).

Of course, the constitutive unity of the Church desired by her Founder has never been lacking.... But it cannot be denied that historically, in the past as in the present, the unity of the Church does not fully show either the vigor or the extension which she could and must achieve in accordance with the requirements of the Gospel.

Thus, the fundamental attitude of Christians who have this unity at heart and who are aware of the gap that exists between the unity desired by Christ and what has concretely been achieved, cannot but be to turn their eyes to heaven, to implore God to provide ever new incentives to unity with the Holy Spirit's inspiration....

If it is to be authentic and fruitful, ecumenism demands from the Catholic faithful some basic attitudes. In the first place charity, with a gaze full of compassion and a sincere desire to cooperate, wherever possible, with our brothers and sisters in the other churches or ecclesial communities; in the second place, fidelity to the Catholic Church while neither disregarding nor denying the visible failings in the conduct of some of her members; in the third place, the spirit of discernment, in order to appreciate what is good and praiseworthy; lastly, a sincere wish for purification and renewal, both through personal commitment oriented to Christian perfection and by contributing "each according to his own station, to play his part, that the Church, which bears in her own body the humility and dying of Jesus (cf. 2 Cor 4:10; Phil 2:5-8), may daily be more purified and renewed, against the day when Christ will present her to himself in all her glory without spot or wrinkle (cf. Eph 5:27)" (*Unitatis Redintegratio*, 4).

FOUR

Women

The most beautiful statement on women by Pope John Paul II is found in the request for forgiveness that is contained in his *Letter to Women* (June, 1995). The most touching expression is found in a passage in the Apostolic Letter, *Vita Consecrata* (March, 1996), which portrays consecrated women as "signs of God's tender love toward the human race" (57). There is also a poetic description in *Mulieris Dignitatem* (September, 1988): "In the biblical description, the words of the first man at the sight of the woman who had been created are words of admiration and enchantment, words which fill the whole history of man on earth" (10).

The boldest stroke is also found in *Mulieris Dignitatem*, which contains a summation of the biblical references to individual women and even corrects two thousand years of interpretation of the passages in St. Paul which describe man as the "head" of the woman. He even corrects St. Paul—or what is based on antiquity in his writings—when he states: "All the reasons in favor of the 'subjection' of woman to man in marriage must be understood in the sense of a 'mutual subjection' of both 'out of reverence for Christ'" (24).

The statements of the Pope are a manifestation of his particular affection for women in the Church. He gives expression to his tenderness with great freedom, and in so doing, he radically revises the traditional papal attitude. Popes have never before been seen (but we hope henceforth to see it regularly) to kiss little girls, hug them, take them by the hand or almost dance with them. Even this change of behavior has been, in its own way, a revision of history.

But it is necessary to tell the whole story about the Pope and women. Hence, we must add that this Pope, so generous in his words and actions, has not made any changes up to this time that would open up new areas of responsibility for women. And he could have done so, even with his firm resolve not to take any steps forward on the question of priestly ordination. For example, the same difficulties do not exist as regards the admission of women to the diaconate.

To put a date on Pope John Paul's interventions and confession of faults concerning the treatment of women, we would say that those which contain an explicit request for forgiveness or an admission of the need for reparation, all took place in 1995, in connection with the International Year of the Woman. Prior to that, of course, he had proposed an examination of conscience at the end of the second millennium in the Apostolic Letter, *Tertio Millennio Adveniente* (November, 1994). On the other hand, there is no explicit mea culpa in the document, *Mulieris Dignitatem* (1988), though there is the hint of a doctrinal revision and a change of attitude.

Correction of St. Paul's Teaching

Here are some passages from *Mulieris Dignitatem* in which Pope John Paul corrects the teaching of St. Paul (something which no pope had ever done) and the traditional teaching in the history of the Church. It has to do with the concept of man as "head of the woman" and the question of Eve's sin:

The biblical description of original sin in the third chapter of Genesis in a certain way "distinguishes the roles" which the woman and the man had in it. This is also referred to later in certain passages of the Bible, for example, Paul's Letter to Timothy: "For Adam was formed first, then Eve; and Adam was not deceived, but the woman was deceived and became a transgressor" (1 Tm 2:13-14). But there is no doubt that independent of this "distinction of roles" in the biblical description, that first sin is the sin of man, created by God as male and female. It is also the sin of the "first parents," to which is connected its hereditary character. In this sense we call it "original sin"....

The author of the Letter to the Ephesians sees no contradiction between an exhortation formulated in this way and the words: "Wives, be subject to your husbands, as to the Lord. For the husband is the head of the wife" (Eph 5:22-23). The author knows that this way of speaking, so profoundly rooted in the customs and religious tradition of the time, is to be understood and carried out in a new way: as a "mutual subjection out of reverence for Christ" (Eph 5:21).... In relation to the "old" this is evidently something "new": it is an innovation of the Gospel. We find various passages in which the apostolic writings express this innovation, even though they also communicate what is "old": what is rooted in the religious tradition of Israel.... However, the awareness that in marriage there is a mutual "subjection of the spouses out of reverence for Christ" and not just that of the wife to the husband must gradually establish itself in hearts, consciences, behaviors and customs. This is a call which from that time onward does not cease to challenge succeeding generations; it is a call which people have to accept ever anew.... All the suggestions in favor of the "subjection" of woman to man in marriage must be understood in the sense of a "mutual subjection" of both "out of reverence for Christ" (*Mulieris Dignitatem*, 9; 24).

The boldness of this reinterpretation of St. Paul's teaching has been recognized by the feminist movement and had previously been requested by theologians favorable to it. This is how it was originally stated by Hans Küng, as early as 1976 (twelve years before Pope John Paul's Apostolic Letter, *Mulieris Dignitatem*: "New Testament statements concerning the subordination of a wife to her husband (mostly found in later New Testament writings) must be understood in their socio-cultural context and present socio-cultural conditions must be taken into account."[37] That is exactly what Pope John Paul has done.

Expression of Regret

The first explicit admission of the historical responsibility of the Church in regard to the treatment of women was expressed by the Pope in June, 1995:

Equality between man and woman is in fact asserted from the first page of the Bible in the stupendous narrative of creation. The Book of Genesis says: "God created man in his own image; in the image of God he created him; male and female he created them" (Gn 1:27).... This original biblical message is fully expressed in Jesus' words and deeds. In his time women were weighed down by an inherited mentality in which they were deeply discriminated. The Lord's attitude was a "consistent protest against whatever offends the dignity of women" (*Mulieris Dignitatem,* 15)....

In the footprints of her divine Founder, the Church becomes the convinced bearer of this message. If down the centuries some of her children have at times not lived it with the same consistency, this is a reason for deep regret. The Gospel message about women, however, has lost none of its timeliness (Sunday Angelus, June 25, 1995).

What a capacity John Paul II has to surprise people! Scarcely three years before asking pardon from women, similar words were placed in the mouth of an imaginary evangelical pope of the future. It is contained in a small book entitled *Confidential Writings of His Holiness John Paul III* by an anonymous Spaniard. Having convoked an Ecumenical Council in Mexico City, this fictional John Paul announces his resignation in the opening session, and among his other imagined statements is this one: "My voice is raised to ask pardon of you, women of the whole world, for the brutality, lack of understanding, disdain, oppression and discrimination that we have practiced against you, mothers, wives, daughters, sisters and family members for so many centuries, down to the present day."

The same expression of regret proposed as a "dream" in 1994 was accompanied by a confession of sin that was formulated and promulgated by the highest authority of the Society of Jesus. In the spring of 1995 the Thirty-fourth General Congregation approved a document on women in which the Jesuits admit that both as men and as men of the Church they have given offense to women: "To answer for that responsibility, we Jesuits first of all ask of God the grace of conversion. We have taken part in a civil and ecclesiastical tradition that has given offence to women. Like many men, we find in ourselves the tendency to tell ourselves that there is no problem. Even without wanting to do so, we have been partners in a form of clericalism which has reinforced male domination, giving it the stamp of divine approval. Recognizing this, we want to react as individuals and as a community and we intend to do everything possible to change this unacceptable situation" (Decree of the General Congregation: "The Jesuits and the status of woman in the Church and in civil society," 1995).

Asking Pardon

The expression of regret becomes an explicit request for forgiveness in the Pope's *Letter to Women,* published in June, 1995:

> Thank you, every woman, for the simple fact of being a woman! Through the insight which is so much a part of your womanhood you enrich the world's understanding and help to make human relations more honest and authentic.
>
> I know of course that simply saying thank you is not enough. Unfortunately, we are heirs to a history which has conditioned us to a remarkable extent. In every time and place this conditioning has been an obstacle to the progress of women. Women's dignity has often been unacknowledged and their prerogatives misrepresented; they have often been relegated to the margins of society and even reduced to servitude.... And if objective blame, especially in particular historical contexts, has belonged to not just a few members of the Church, for this I am truly sorry. May this regret be transformed, on the part of the whole Church, into a renewed commitment of fidelity to the Gospel vision.
>
> When it comes to setting women free from every kind of exploitation and domination, the Gospel con-

tains an ever relevant message which goes back to the attitude of Jesus Christ himself. Transcending the established norms of his own culture, Jesus treated women with openness, respect, acceptance and tenderness. In this way he honored the dignity which women have always possessed according to God's plan and in his love. As we look to Christ at the end of this second millennium, it is natural to ask ourselves how much of his message has been heard and acted upon.

Yes, it is time to examine the past with courage, to assign responsibility where it is due in a review of the long history of humanity. Women have contributed to that history as much as men, and more often than not they did so in much more difficult conditions.... To this great, immense feminine "tradition" humanity owes a debt which can never be repaid. Yet how many women have been and continue to be valued more for their physical appearance than for their skill, their professionalism, their intellectual abilities, their deep sensitivity; in a word, the very dignity of their being! (*Letter to Women,* June 29, 1995).

When the document *Mulieris Dignitatem* was published in 1988, one of the criticisms was: "It lacks any suggestion of self-examination and confession of guilt; and this is typical of official Catholic documents"; and also: "The pope gives thanks but he neglects to ask forgiveness." But no one can say that today. From what we have seen thus far, the Catholic documents issued under Pope John Paul II are not lacking in self-examination or in requests for forgiveness. And not even ten years have passed since such criticisms were quite common!

Rewriting History

When discussing the treatment of women, and also when discussing ecumenism (as we shall do in Chapter

19), the admission of historical responsibility should lead logically to the need to rewrite history. This was explicitly stated by Pope John Paul:

> In the message which, last May 26, I addressed to Mrs. Gertrude Mongella, Secretary General of the forthcoming Beijing Conference, I made the observation that because of a new appreciation of woman's role in society, it would be appropriate to rewrite history in a less one-sided way. Unfortunately, a certain way of writing history has paid greater attention to extraordinary and sensational events than to the daily rhythm of life, and the resulting history is almost only concerned with the achievements of men. This tendency should be reversed. How much still needs to be said and written about man's enormous debt to woman in every other realm of social and cultural progress! With the intention of helping to fill this gap, I would like to speak on behalf of the Church and to pay homage to the manifold, immense, although frequently silent, contribution of women in every area of human life (Sunday Angelus, July 30, 1995).

Favoring Participation of Women

Here is a text that demonstrates the novelty and the extent of the Pope's attitude toward women in the Church. He realizes that women should be more highly appreciated, thus admitting that the situation is defective; nevertheless he does not see any need to correct the situation by means of a reform. Rather, he advises the full use of the ample resources that are already available:

> Today I appeal to the whole Church community to be willing to foster feminine participation in every way in its internal life.... The Church is increasingly aware of the need for enhancing their role.... The 1987 Synod

on the laity expressed precisely this need and asked that "without discrimination women should be participants in the life of the Church and also in consultation and the process of coming to decisions" (*Propositio* 47; cf. *Christifideles Laici,* 51).

This is the way to be courageously taken. To a large extent, it is a question of making full use of the ample room for a lay and feminine presence recognized by the Church's law. I am thinking, for example, of theological teaching, the forms of the liturgical ministry permitted, including service at the altar, pastoral and administrative councils, diocesan synods and particular councils, various ecclesial institutions, Curias, and ecclesiastical tribunals, many pastoral activities, including the new forms of participation in the care of parishes when there is a shortage of clergy, except for those tasks that belong properly to the priest. Who can imagine the great advantages to pastoral care and the new beauty that the Church's face will assume, when the feminine genius is fully involved in the various areas of her life? (Sunday Angelus, September 3, 1995).

The Consecrated Woman

In the following passage the Pope states that the full acceptance of women in the Church will contribute greatly to the discontinuance of the "one-sided vision" of the history and activity of the Church. This self-examination is immediately evident in the language that the Pope uses:

It is equally important to point out that women's new self-awareness also helps men to reconsider their way of looking at things, the way they understand themselves, where they place themselves in history and how they interpret it and the way they organize social, political, economic, religious and ecclesial life.... In this context the consecrated woman, on the basis of her experience of the Church and as a woman in the Church, can help eliminate certain one-sided perspectives which do not fully recognize her dignity and her specific contribution to the Church's life and pastoral and missionary activity. Consecrated women therefore rightly aspire to have their identity, ability, mission and responsibility more clearly recognized, both in the awareness of the Church and in everyday life.... It is therefore urgently necessary to take certain concrete steps, beginning by providing room for women to participate in different fields and at all levels, including decision-making processes, above all in matters which concern women themselves (Apostolic Letter, *Vita Consecrata,* March, 1996).

FIVE

The Jews

Pope John Paul II has much to say to the Jews, both in words and in deeds, but he has not yet made an explicit request for forgiveness. Nevertheless, he has called them "our elder brothers"; he has visited their synagogue in Rome; he has established diplomatic relations between the Vatican and the State of Israel. On numerous occasions he has admitted the historical responsibility of the Church for the persecution of Jews. When he spoke at the synagogue in Rome, he deplored the discrimination against the Jews at the hands of his predecessors in the papacy. He also authorized a prayer in St. Peter's Basilica asking God's forgiveness for the indifference of Christians to the Holocaust during the Nazi regime.

But an explicit and direct request for forgiveness has not been forthcoming. Nor did the Second Vatican Council make any such request, although the request for pardon has been suggested and solicited numerous times. The material gathered together in this chapter will demonstrate that the time is ripe for such a gesture and everything prompts us to think that it should come from Pope John Paul II, as a right more than as a duty.

Our Elder Brothers

When he visited the synagogue in Rome in April of 1986, Pope Wojtyla, quoting the Second Vatican Council, deplored the "displays of anti-Semitism leveled at any time or from any source against the Jews." And he repeated the phrase "from any source" with emphasis, which some have interpreted as an admission of papal responsibility:

> This gathering in a way brings to a close, after the Pontificate of John XXIII and the Second Vatican Council, a long period which we must not tire of reflecting upon in order to draw from it the appropriate lessons. Certainly, we cannot and should not forget that the historical circumstances of the past were very different from those that have laboriously matured over the centuries. The general acceptance of a legitimate plurality on the social, civil and religious levels has been arrived at with great difficulty. Nevertheless, a consideration of centuries-long cultural conditioning could not prevent us from recognizing that the acts of discrimination, unjustified limitation of religious freedom, oppression also on the level of civil freedom in regard to the Jews were, from an objective point of view, gravely deplorable manifestations. Yes, once again, through myself, the Church, in the words of the well-known Declaration *Nostra Aetate* (4), "deplores the hatred, persecutions, and displays of anti-Semitism directed against the Jews at any time and by anyone"; I repeat: "by anyone."
>
> I would like once more to express a word of abhorrence for the genocide decreed against the Jewish people during the last War, which led to the holocaust of millions of innocent victims.... The Jewish community of Rome too paid a high price in blood. And it was surely a significant gesture that in those dark years of racial persecution the doors of our religious houses, of our churches, of the Roman Seminary, of buildings be-

longing to the Holy See and of Vatican City itself were thrown open to offer refuge and safety to so many Jews of Rome being hunted by their persecutors.

Today's visit is meant to make a decisive contribution to the consolidation of the good relations between our two communities, in imitation of the example of so many men and women who have worked and are still working today, on both sides, to overcome old prejudices and to secure ever wider and fuller recognition of that "bond" and that "common spiritual patrimony" that exists between Jews and Christians.

This is the hope expressed in the fourth paragraph of the Council's Declaration *Nostra Aetate,* which I have just mentioned, on the relationship of the Church to non-Christian religions. The decisive turning-point in relations between the Catholic Church and Judaism, and with individual Jews, was occasioned by this brief but incisive paragraph (Visit to the Synagogue in Rome, April 13, 1986).

How Could We Not Be With You?

We are in St. Peter's Square. It is April 13, 1993, and the Pope is recalling, at a distance of fifty years, the days of the *Sho'ah,* one of "history's darkest nights." He assures the Jews that they are not the only ones to experience the pain of this memory. There is a strong—one could say insistent—implication that the Jews were left all alone by Christians to endure those terrible events:

> The joy of this day must not prevent us from turning our attention to an event, so filled with human suffering, which took place 50 years ago: the uprising in the Warsaw ghetto. I feel a great need to greet all those, Christians and Jews, who have come to this square to commemorate that fact and the crimes perpetrated against the Jewish people during the last World War.

In deep solidarity with that people, and in communion with the whole community of Catholics, I would like to commemorate those terrible events, so remote in time, but etched in the minds of many of us. The days of the *Sho'ah* marked one of "history's darkest nights," with unimaginable crimes against God and humanity. How could we not be with you, dear Jewish brothers and sisters, to recall in prayer and meditation, such a tragic anniversary? Be sure of this: you are not alone in bearing the pain of this memory; we pray and watch with you, under the gaze of God, the holy and just one, rich in mercy and pardon (St. Peter's, April 18, 1993).

Sorrow for Past Indifference

The following words from the summer of 1987 are the most specific expression of repentance for the persecutions of the past:

There is no doubt that the sufferings inflicted upon the Jews are also for the Catholic Church a reason for deep sorrow, especially if we think of the indifference and sometimes the resentment that in particular historical situations have divided the Jews and Christians. Certainly this calls for yet stronger resolutions to cooperate for justice and true peace (Letter to the President of the Conference of Bishops of the United States, August, 1987).

The admission of blame was taken up again, but not surpassed, in an address nine years later:

The Declaration *Nostra Aetate* contains a special reference to our Jewish brethren, with whom Christianity has an especially close relationship. In fact, the Christian religion has its origin in the religious experience of the Hebrew people, from whom Christ came forth according to the flesh. Sharing with the Jews the part of Scripture that goes by the name of the Old Testament, the Church continues to live that same patrimony of truth, rereading it in the light of Christ. The inauguration of the new age established by him with a new and eternal Covenant, does not destroy the ancient foundation but opens it up to universal fruitfulness. Considering all that, the remembrance of the tensions that have so often marked the relationship between Christians and Jews cannot help but arouse great sorrow (Sunday Angelus, January 14, 1996).

Indifference to the Holocaust

Christians were certainly responsible or co-responsible for the persecutions of the Jews in past history. The extent to which they were responsible for the Holocaust during the regime of Hitler is a moot point, but they are certainly guilty of remaining passive and for the most part indifferent. That much has been admitted in a papal statement. We refer to the prayer recited by Pope John Paul II at the ecumenical celebration in St. Peter's to mark the close of the European Synod in 1991. It is a prayer that asks forgiveness for the indifference of Christians in the face of the Holocaust, perhaps the most explicit text authorized by the present Pope:

> Lord, our Liberator, we of the Christian communities of Europe have not always obeyed your precept but, relying only on human power, we have followed worldly prudence with wars of religion, with struggles of Christians against Christians, with indifference in the face of persecutions and the Holocaust of the Jews, with furious attacks against so many of the just. Pardon us and have mercy on us! (Prayer at the ecumenical service marking the end of the European Synod, December 7, 1991).

The opportunity to ask forgiveness from the Jews has frequently been noted by high-ranking authorities in the Church. We note first of all the statement of Cardinal Bea, who said in a conference in 1964: "We should perhaps also confess here many faults of the Church. You know what the Holy Father Paul VI has said regarding the division among Christians: 'If among the causes of this division any fault can be imputed to us, we humbly beg God's forgiveness and we also ask pardon from the brethren who feel that they have been offended by us.' This statement made a great impression on Protestants, and the same can be said of the reaction of the Jews. The Church, and especially the sons of the Church, the Christians, have committed injustices against the Jewish people. We can admit this without any offence against the truth."[38]

Twenty years later, at the Extraordinary Synod of 1985, Cardinal Willebrands recalled with deep emotion the new relationship between Catholics and Jews that was inaugurated by the Second Vatican Council: "It asked for a radical change and it has been practically a miracle." He admitted, however, that two decades are not enough "to overcome the mutual ignorance and the social and religious indifference that has accumulated through the centuries." After this admission, the Cardinal touched on the need to ask for forgiveness: "Among the persecutors there were also Christians, sometimes even believing that they were acting out of religious motives."

This courageous Cardinal was asked during a press conference on December 3, 1985, why the Synod did not ask for forgiveness from the Jews for the past behavior of the Church in various confrontations. He honestly admitted the need for such a request, but perhaps the time has not yet arrived: "A declaration of repentance is meaningful only in a climate of mutual trust between Christians and Jews. We have increased the trust between the Jews and ourselves, but there is still a great deal of uncertainty as to whether an initiative of this kind can be proposed and accepted."[39]

Cardinal Willebrands, the successor to Cardinal Bea, was a valiant fighter on all fronts in the field of ecumenism, on Luther, on the Jews and on the Russian Orthodox Church. And his successor, Cardinal Cassidy, is no less so. He has stated on a solemn occasion in Prague in September of 1990, at the conclusion of a meeting of the International Committee on Jewish and Christian relations, that the goal of the Catholic discussions on relations with Judaism is to arrive at a request for forgiveness: "The fact that anti-Semitism has found a place in the Christian conscience and practice calls for an act of *teshuvà* (repentance and conversion) and reconciliation."[40]

An attitude similar to that of Cardinal Willebrands and Cardinal Cassidy is held today by Cardinal Etchegaray, who is perhaps the most impassioned man in the entire Curia! His most impressive words on the Jews are in an explicit proposal for a request for forgiveness, which he stated before he became a member of the Curia. He was speaking at that time as Archbishop of Marseilles at the Synod of 1983, and he concluded by asking pardon for having the audacity to bring up the Jewish question. Then he said: "As long as Judaism remains foreign to our history of salvation, we shall be influenced by anti-Semitic attitudes. We also have a need for repentance because of our secular attitude toward the Jewish people. It is necessary for us to know how to ask pardon of the Lord and of our brethren. It is necessary to pledge ourselves to repair what needs to be re-paired."[41] Cardinal Etchegaray spoke those words on October 5, 1983. Six months later he was called to serve in the Curia at Rome, and ten years after that he was named to preside over the committee for the Great Jubilee. I like to think that the Pope's trust in him stems in great part from the words we have just quoted.

Something equivalent to a request for forgiveness from the Jews was expressed by the Spanish bishops and published in *L'Osservatore Romano* on March 31, 1992. The text was read by Archbishop Torella Cascante to a conference of Jewish rabbis from America, held at Toledo, Spain: "There is no doubt that what the Christians did to the Jews and Muslims in Spain in 1492 was exactly the opposite of what should have been done in accordance with our Christian faith. People today think differently. We should not judge, but we can and we ought to deplore what was done. 1492 was a period of persecution, rejection, expulsion, forced conversion, exile and death. The fact that the same year marks the beginning of the great adventure of modern times, the opening of Europe to the Americas, does not change the picture very much. Instead, it makes it more painful. The same men and women were responsible for both of these things."

Self-criticism for the Holocaust has been much more explicit among the Protestants than among the Catholics. In all the documents that we have cited and among all the Vatican personnel and conferences of bishops, we have not found any clear and precise confession of sin comparable to that contained in a declaration by the Evangelical Church of the Rhineland, published in January, 1980: "We confess that we, as German Christians, are also responsible and at fault for the Holocaust."[42]

For no other chapter in this book, not even for the one on Galileo, is there such an accumulation of evidence for the need of historical revision as for this one on the Jews. And it is not yet finished. The vastness of the testimony and the delay in acceding to the request for forgiveness are an indication of the importance of the response we are waiting for.

SIX

Galileo

The importance of the Galileo case stems from the fact that it marks the encounter between the Church and the modern age, and the review of its history has inspired the reflection that led to the proposal for an examination of conscience at the end of the present millennium. We present here the three basic texts relating to the self-examination: the one in which the Pope requested it, in November of 1979, a year after his election to the papal throne; the one in which Cardinal Poupard, thirteen years later, summarized the faults which the Church admits; and the one in which the Pope replied to Cardinal Poupard's report and suggested other applications to the rapport between faith and science, as a result of the re-examination of the Galileo case.

Reopening the Galileo Case

The Pope announced the re-examination of the Galileo case at a meeting with the Pontifical Academy of the Sciences in a ceremony commemorating Albert Einstein in November, 1979. There is no mea culpa in this book that is earlier than this one. The Galileo case was taken up by the Second Vatican Council, which made amends without mentioning Galileo's name. The passage is found in *Gaudium et Spes* (1965), and we shall see it in the allocution by Pope John Paul II in memory of Albert Einstein. The decision to return to the Galileo case indicates a dissatisfaction with the act of reparation by the Second Vatican Council and the slight impact that it made. At the same time, it reveals the Pope's confidence that everything can be clarified and every misunderstanding corrected:

> The greatness of Galileo is known to everyone, like that of Einstein: but unlike the latter, whom we are honoring today before the College of Cardinals in the apostolic palace, the former had to suffer a great deal—we cannot conceal the fact—at the hands of men and organisms of the Church. The Second Vatican Council recognized and deplored certain unwarranted interventions: "We cannot but deplore"—it is written in number 36 of the Conciliar Constitution *Gaudium et Spes*—"certain attitudes (not unknown among Christians) deriving from a shortsighted view of the rightful autonomy of science: they have occasioned conflict and controversy and have misled many into thinking that faith and science are opposed." The reference to Galileo is clearly expressed in the note to this text, which cites the volume *Vita e Opere di Galileo Galilei* by Monsignor Pio Paschini, published by the Pontifical Academy of Sciences.
>
> To go beyond this stand taken by the Council, I hope that theologians, scholars and historians, animated by a spirit of sincere collaboration, will study the Galileo case more deeply and, in loyal recognition of wrongs from whatever side they come, will dispel the mistrust that still opposes, in many minds, a fruitful concord between science and faith, between the Church and the world. I give all my support to this

task, which will be able to honor the truth of faith and of science and open the door to future collaboration (Apostolic Palace, November 10, 1979).

Cardinal Poupard's Report

This report is so important that we shall copy it in its entirety. It was read in French by Cardinal Poupard, head of the commission for the study of the Galileo case, on October 31, 1992, to the Pontifical Academy of Sciences and in the presence of Pope John Paul II.

Some critics noted that in paragraph five, and in italics, the Cardinal referred to "Galileo's judges" when he should have said "the Holy Office." Similar observations were made about the papal text because of the expressions "theologians who opposed him" and "theologians of the time" instead of "the authority of the Church." However, Cardinal Poupard did state explicitly early in his report that the purpose of the research was to explore the difficult relations of Galileo with the Church; and in the fourth paragraph of our quotation from the Holy Father he states that "the Church has the duty to be attentive to the pastoral consequences of her teaching" and her pastors should avoid the "double trap of a hesitant attitude and of hasty judgment."

The second paragraph of section five of Cardinal Poupard's report, on the other hand, could serve very well as a model for future admissions of responsibility. The phrase "had much to suffer" is taken from the papal text mentioned above, but let us look at the entire report by Cardinal Poupard:

Most Holy Father,

Nearly thirteen years have now passed since you received the Pontifical Academy of Sciences, in this same Sala Regia, for the first centenary of the birth of Albert

Einstein, and again directed the attention of the world of culture and of science to another scholar, Galileo Galilei.

1. You expressed the hope that interdisciplinary research would be undertaken to explore the difficult relations of Galileo with the Church. You also established, on July 3, 1981, a Pontifical Commission for the study of the Ptolemaic-Copernican controversy of the 16th and 17th centuries, to which the Galileo case belongs, and you had entrusted to Cardinal Garrone responsibility for coordinating the research. You have asked me to give an account of their results.

That Commission was made up of four working groups, with the following chairmen: Cardinal Carlo Martini for the exegetical section; myself for the cultural section; Professor Carlos Chagas and Father George Coyne for the scientific and epistemological section; Monsignor Michele Maccarone for historical and juridical questions; Father Enrico di Rovasenda served as secretary.

The aim of these groups was to reply to the expectations of the world of science and culture regarding the Galileo question, to rethink this whole question, with complete fidelity to established historical facts and in conformity with the teachings and the culture of the times, and to recognize honestly, in the spirit of the Second Vatican Council, the rights and the wrongs, regardless of their source. It was not a question of conducting a retrial but of undertaking a calm and objective reflection, taking into account the historical and cultural context. The investigation was broad, exhaustive and carried out in all the areas involved. And the series of studies, theses and publications of the Commission have also stimulated numerous studies in various spheres.

2. The Commission addressed three questions: What happened? How did it happen? Why did it happen?

The answers to these three questions, answers based upon a critical investigation of the texts, throw light on a number of important points.

The critical edition of the documents, and in particular of items from the Vatican Secret Archives, enables one to consult easily and with all the desirable guarantees the complete record of the two trials and especially the detailed accounts of the interrogations to which Galileo was subjected. The publication of Cardinal Bellarmine's declaration to Galileo, together with that of other documents, clarifies the intellectual horizon of that key person of the whole affair. The editing and publication of a series of studies have cast light on the cultural, philosophical and theological context of the 17th century. They have also led to a clearer understanding of the positions taken by Galileo with respect to the decrees of the Council of Trent and to the exegetical orientations of his time, and this has made possible a careful appraisal of the immense literature dedicated to Galileo, from the Enlightenment down to our own day.

Cardinal Robert Bellarmine, in a letter of April 12, 1615, to the Carmelite Foscarini, had already stated the two real questions raised by Copernicus's system: is Copernican astronomy true, in the sense that it is supported by real and verifiable proofs, or does it rest only on conjectures or probabilities? Are the Copernican theses compatible with the statements of Sacred Scripture? According to Robert Bellarmine, as long as there was no proof that the earth orbited round the sun, it was necessary to interpret with great circumspection the biblical passages declaring the earth to be immobile. If the orbiting of the earth were ever demonstrated to be certain, then theologians, according to him, would have to review their interpretations of the biblical passages that are apparently opposed to the new Copernican theories, in order to avoid defining as erroneous any opinions which had been proved to be true: "I say that if it were really demonstrated that the sun is at the center of the world and the earth is in the third heaven, and that it is not the sun which revolves round the earth, but the earth round the sun, then it would be necessary to proceed with great circumspection in the explanation of scriptural texts which seem contrary to this assertion and to say that we do not understand them, rather than to say that what is demonstrated is false."

3. In fact, Galileo had not succeeded in proving irrefutably the double motion of the earth—its annual orbit round the sun and its daily rotation on the polar axis—when he was convinced that he had found proof of it in the ocean tides, the true origin of which only Newton would later demonstrate. Galileo proposed tentative proof in the existence of the trade winds, but at that time no one had the knowledge necessary for drawing therefrom the necessary clarifications.

More than 150 years still had to pass before the optical and mechanical proofs for the motion of the earth were discovered. For their part, Galileo's adversaries, neither before nor after him, have discovered anything which could constitute a convincing refutation of Copernican astronomy. The facts were unavoidably clear, and they soon showed the relative character of the sentence passed in 1633. This sentence was not irreformable. In 1741, in the face of the optical proof of the fact that the earth revolves round the sun, Benedict XIV had the Holy Office grant an imprimatur to the first edition of *The Complete Works of Galileo*.

4. This implicit reform of the 1633 sentence became explicit in the Decree of the Sacred Congregation of the Index, which removed from the 1757 edition of the *Index of Forbidden Books*, works favoring the heliocentric theory. Despite this decree, however, there were many who remained hesitant about admitting the new inter-

pretation. In 1820, Canon Settele, Professor at the University of Rome La Sapienza, was preparing to publish his *Elements of Optics and Astronomy*. He came up against the refusal of Father Anfossi, Master of the Sacred Palace, to grant the imprimatur. This incident gave the impression that the 1633 sentence had indeed remained unreformed because it was irreformable. The unjustly censured author lodged an appeal with Pope Pius VII, from whom in 1822 he received a favorable decision. A decisive fact was this: Father Olivieri, former Master General of the Order of Preachers and Commissary of the Holy Office, drew up a report favoring the granting of the imprimatur to works presenting Copernican astronomy as a thesis, and no longer as a mere hypothesis.

This papal decision was to receive its practical application in 1846, with the publication of a new and updated *Index*.

5. In conclusion, a rereading of the archival documents shows once more that all those involved in the trial, without exception, have a right to the benefit of good faith, in the absence of extra-procedural documents showing the contrary. The philosophical and theological qualifications wrongly granted to the then new theories about the centrality of the sun and the movement of the earth were the result of a transitional situation in the field of astronomical knowledge, and of an exegetical confusion regarding cosmology. Certain theologians, Galileo's contemporaries, being heirs of a unitary concept of the world universally accepted until the dawn of the 17th century, failed to grasp the profound, non-literal meaning of the Scriptures when they describe the physical structure of the created universe. This led them unduly to transpose a question of factual observation into the realm of faith.

It is in that historical and cultural framework, far removed from our own times, that Galileo's judges, incapable of dissociating faith from an age-old cosmology, believed quite wrongly that the adoption of the Copernican revolution, in fact not yet definitively proven, was such as to undermine Catholic tradition, and that it was their duty to forbid its being taught. This subjective error of judgment, so clear to us today, led them to a disciplinary measure from which Galileo "had much to suffer." These mistakes must be frankly recognized, as you, Holy Father, have requested.

These are the results of the interdisciplinary inquiry which you asked the Commission to undertake. All its members, through myself, thank you for the honor and trust which you have shown to them in leaving them the fullest latitude to explore, research and publish, in the complete freedom which scientific studies demand. May Your Holiness deign to accept the Commission's fervent and filial homage.

Paul Cardinal Poupard
Città del Vaticano
October 31, 1992

Pope Wojtyla Acknowledges the Mistakes

We have already mentioned the importance that Pope John Paul placed on the pastoral question in his response to the report by Cardinal Poupard at the official session of the Pontifical Academy of Sciences. Equally explicit are the expressions "tragic mutual incomprehension," "sad misunderstanding," and "error of the theologians of the time," which are found in the allocution of Pope John Paul which we shall now quote in part:

One might perhaps be surprised that, at the end of the Academy's study week on the theme of the emergence of complexity in the various sciences, I am returning to the Galileo case. Has not this case long been shelved and have not the errors committed been recognized?

That is certainly true. However, the underlying problems of this case concern both the nature of science and the message of faith. It is therefore not to be excluded that one day we shall find ourselves in a similar situation, one which will require both sides to have an informed awareness of the field and of the limits of their own competencies. The approach provided by the theme of complexity could provide an illustration of this.

A twofold question is at the heart at the debate of which Galileo was the center. The first is of the epistemological order and concerns biblical hermeneutics.... The problem posed by theologians of that age was, therefore, that of the compatibility between heliocentrism and Scripture. Thus the new science, with its methods and the freedom of research which they implied, obliged theologians to examine their own criteria of scriptural interpretation. Most of them did not know how to do so.

Paradoxically, Galileo, a sincere believer, showed himself to be more perceptive in this regard than the theologians who opposed him. "If Scripture cannot err," he wrote to Benedetto Castelli, "certain of its interpreters and commentators can and do so in many ways."

From this we can now draw our first conclusion. The birth of a new way of approaching the study of natural phenomena demands a clarification on the part of all disciplines of knowledge. It obliges them to define more clearly their own field, their approach, their methods, as well as the precise import of their conclusions. In other words, this new way requires each discipline to become more rigorously aware of its own nature.

The upset caused by the Copernican system thus demanded epistemological reflection on the biblical sciences, an effort which later would produce abundant fruit in modern exegetical works and which has found sanction and a new stimulus in the Dogmatic Constitution *Dei Verbum* of the Second Vatican Council.

The crisis that I have just recalled is not the only factor to have had repercussions on biblical interpretation. Here we are concerned with the second aspect of the problem, its pastoral dimension. By virtue of her own mission, the Church has the duty to be attentive to the pastoral consequences of her teaching. Before all else, let it be clear that this teaching must correspond to the truth. But it is a question of knowing how to judge a new scientific datum when it seems to contradict the truths of faith. The pastoral judgment which the Copernican theory required was difficult to make insofar as geocentrism seemed to be a part of scriptural teaching itself. It would have been necessary all at once to overcome habits of thought and to devise a way of teaching capable of enlightening the people of God. Let us say, in a general way, that the pastor ought to show a genuine boldness, avoiding the double trap of a hesitant attitude and of hasty judgment, both of which can cause considerable harm....

From the beginning of the Age of Enlightenment down to our own day, the Galileo case has been a sort of "myth," in which the image fabricated out of the events was quite far removed from reality. In this perspective, the Galileo case was the symbol of the Church's supposed rejection of scientific progress, or of dogmatic "obscurantism" opposed to the free search for truth. This myth has played a considerable cultural role. It has helped to anchor a number of scientists of good faith in the idea that there was an incompatibility between the spirit of science and its rules of research on the one hand and the Christian faith on the other. A tragic mutual incomprehension has been interpreted as the reflection of a fundamental opposition between science and faith. The clarifications provided by recent historical studies enable us to state that this sad misunderstanding now belongs to the past.

From the Galileo affair we can learn a lesson which remains valid in relation to similar situations which occur today and which may occur in the future. In Galileo's time, to depict the world as lacking an absolute physical reference point was, so to speak, inconceivable. And since the cosmos, as it was then known, was contained within the solar system alone, this reference point could only be situated in the earth or in the sun. Today, after Einstein and within the perspective of contemporary cosmology, neither of these two reference points has the importance they once had. This observation, it goes without saying, is not directed against the validity of Galileo's position in the debate; it is only meant to show that often, beyond two partial and conflicting perceptions, there exists a wider perception which includes them and goes beyond both of them.

Another lesson which we can draw is that the different branches of knowledge call for different methods. Thanks to his intuition as a brilliant physicist and by relying on different arguments, Galileo, who practically invented the experimental method, understood why only the sun could function as the center of the world, as it was then known, that is to say, as a planetary system. The error of the theologians of the time, when they maintained the centrality of the earth, was to think that our understanding of the physical world's structure was, in some way, imposed by the literal sense of Sacred Scripture (Address to the Pontifical Academy of Sciences, Apostolic Palace, October 31, 1992).

To clarify the Pope's description of the Galileo case as a "sort of myth," Father Georges Cottier, OP, theologian of the papal household, made this observation:

One cannot use the tenacious persistence of a tendentious myth as evidence against a fact of history. An example of this is the Galileo case. There were errors and omissions on the part of responsible ecclesiastics, but later they have been identified and admitted. But as regards the case itself, after the century of Enlightenment, a myth of "scientistic" inspiration grew up around the case, pitting the dogmatic "obscurantism" of the Church against the champions of freedom of thought. If they persist, myths of this type acquire a sort of autonomy, as if to free themselves from the reality of the facts on which they based their origin. In this respect, it shows that we pay a great deal of attention to the pseudo-historical images carried by the mass media.[43]

An Overture to Evolution

When discussing the Galileo case, Pope John Paul stated a fundamental principle concerning the use of Scripture in scientific questions: "It is necessary to define correctly the proper sense of Scripture, rejecting the introduction of interpretations that make it say what it never intended to say." This principle was given a new application in the autumn of 1996, in reference to the theory of evolution. The topic for discussion by the plenary assembly of the Pontifical Academy of Sciences at that time was "The Origins and the Early Evolution of Life: Reflections on Science at the Dawn of the Third Millennium." The Pope sent a message which updates the position of the Church as regards the teaching on evolution:

> Taking into account the state of scientific research at the time as well as the requirements of theology, the Encyclical *Humani Generis* considered the doctrine of "evolutionism" a serious hypothesis, worthy of investigation and in-depth study equal to that of the opposing hypothesis....
>
> Today, almost half a century after the publication of the Encyclical, new knowledge has led to the recog-

nition of more than one hypothesis in the theory of evolution. It is indeed remarkable that this theory has been progressively accepted by researchers, following a series of discoveries in various fields of knowledge. The convergence, neither sought nor fabricated, of the results of work that was conducted independently is in itself a significant argument in favor of this theory....

And, to tell the truth, rather than the theory of evolution, we should speak of several theories of evolution. On the one hand, this plurality has to do with the different explanations advanced for the mechanism of evolution, and on the other, with the various philosophies on which it is based. Hence the existence of materialist, reductionist and spiritualist interpretations. What is to be decided here is the true role of philosophy and, beyond it, of theology....

Consequently, theories of evolution which, in accordance with the philosophies inspiring them, consider the mind as emerging from the forces of living matter, or as a mere epiphenomenon of this matter, are incompatible with the truth about man (Message to the Pontifical Academy of Sciences, October 23, 1996).

SEVEN

War and Peace

Perhaps no other pope has ever preached on peace with the energy of Pope Wojtyla; at least, none in this modern age. And no pope has ever confessed the sin of war committed by Christians and asked for forgiveness as he has done. He seems almost to have exceeded the limits in confessing responsibility and asking pardon, as if Christians were also responsible for wars that were initiated by others, because they did not prevent them or because they took part in them. We shall transcribe the five texts that are the most pertinent as regards the confession of responsibility and the request for forgiveness. The texts extend from 1983 to 1995, beginning at Vienna, one of the great capitals responsible for so many wars between Christian nations; then we pass on to the days at Assisi (1986 and 1993), the symbolic region of Christian dedication to peace; culminating finally in two documents that commemorate the outbreak and the conclusion of the Second World War (1989 and 1995). Pope John Paul considered the Second World War to be the most atrocious scandal in history because it was waged on a continent permeated with Christian traditions.

War as a Compendium of All Sins

Under this aspect, war enfolds all the evils that man has done to man in the history of Europe, and it is "depressing," says the Pope, that "we Christians" have not been any different than others in this respect:

> Nobody can be oblivious of the fact—a fact which deeply affects us all—that the common history of Europe is marked not only by glorious achievements but also by dark and terrifying events which are incompatible with the spirit of humanity and the Gospel of Jesus Christ. Time and again nations and factions full of hatred have waged cruel wars against one another. Time and again people have been deprived of their homes; they have been driven into exile or forced to flee from misery, discrimination and persecution. Millions of people have been killed, on grounds of their race, their nationality, their convictions, or simply because they were deemed undesirable. It is a depressing thought that devout Christians were among those who oppressed and persecuted their fellow human beings....
>
> While we may justly glory in our Lord Jesus Christ and his message, we have, on the other hand, to confess—and ask forgiveness for the fact—that we Christians have burdened ourselves with great guilt—in thoughts, words and deeds, and by not standing up against injustice....
>
> Above all, however, we understand that the language of arms is not the language of Jesus Christ, nor of his Mother, who—then as now—was invoked as the "Help of Christians." Armed combat is, at best, an inevitable ill in which even Christians may be tragically and inevitably involved. But here, too, we are under the Christian obligation to love our enemies, to be merciful (Discourse at Heldenplatz, Vienna, September 10, 1983).

As regards the Pope's incisive comment on armed conflict as an "inevitable evil" and on the love of neighbor that should accompany it, we recall a confession of sin that was the most unexpected in his entire pontificate. I refer to the confession made at Vendée, France, in September, 1996, in reference to the armed resistance of the Catholics of Vendée against the troops sent by the Convention of the Revolution in 1793:

> In the terrible struggles, many deeds on both sides were stained by sin (*L'Osservatore Romano,* September 25, 1996).

The Confession at Assisi

The central event on the day of peace at Assisi in 1986 was the solemn and public confession of responsibility of Catholics and persons of all faiths as participants in the Second World War:

> I humbly repeat here my own conviction: peace bears the name of Jesus Christ. But, at the same time and in the same breath, I am ready to acknowledge that Catholics have not always been faithful to this affirmation of faith. We have not always been "peacemakers." For ourselves, therefore, but also perhaps, in a sense, for all, this encounter at Assisi is an act of penance (Closing address at Assisi, October 27, 1986).

Is Europe Christian?

In the first text cited above, Pope Wojtyla admitted sadly that many Christians had been responsible for the wars in Europe throughout history. He was referring to all the wars in the history of Europe. But in this quotation he is referring to the Second World War, and he is so greatly moved by its intense ferocity that with such a history behind him, he finds it difficult to move forward. Those who insist that this Catholic Pope is not able to make an examination of conscience and an admission of fault should meditate on this passage:

> In conclusion, I wish to address in a special way the pastors and faithful of the Catholic Church.
>
> We have just recalled one of the bloodiest wars in history, a war which broke out on a continent with a Christian tradition. Acknowledgment of this fact compels us to make an examination of conscience about the quality of Europe's evangelization. The collapse of Christian values that led to yesterday's moral failures must make us vigilant as to the way the Gospel is proclaimed and lived out today (Apostolic Letter marking the 50th anniversary of the outbreak of the Second World War, August 26, 1989).

Forgiveness for Us and for All

The prayer asking for God's pardon for today's wars, and not only for wars of the past, was pronounced on the second day at Assisi. It follows the questions as to how it is possible to have enmity in the world if Christ has destroyed enmity and how it is still possible repeatedly to kill one another in the very heart of Europe (the reference is to the former Yugoslavia) when we are at the threshold of the third millennium:

> There is no other answer to such questions but a humble request for pardon for ourselves and for all. It is precisely for this reason that our prayer vigil is also a vigil of penance, of conversion (Prayer vigil for peace in Europe, Assisi, January 9, 1993).

A Mea Culpa for the War Waged by Hitler

It was not precisely the Christians who willed the madness of the Second World War, but the war was waged in Christian lands, and they did not know how to contain it although they participated in it. Consequently, they must ask also for forgiveness for that war. These are courageous words, spoken by a Pole who was nineteen years old when the fury of Hitler turned his life upside down:

> Many are the voices raised on this 50th anniversary of the end of the Second World War in an effort to overcome the divisions between victors and the vanquished. There are commemorations of the courage and sacrifice of millions of men and women. For her part, the Church wishes to listen in particular to the plea of all the victims. It is a plea which helps us understand better the scandal of those six years of conflict. It is a plea which asks us to reflect on what the war meant for all humanity. It is a plea which serves as a renunciation of the ideologies which led to that immense catastrophe.
>
> In the face of every war, we are all called to ponder our responsibilities, to forgive and to ask forgiveness. We feel bitter regret, as Christians, when we consider that "the horrors of that war took place on a continent which could claim a remarkable flowering of culture and civilization—the continent which had remained so long in the light of the Gospel and of the Church." For this the Christians of Europe need to ask forgiveness, even while recognizing that there were varying degrees of responsibility in the events which led to the war (Message marking the 50th anniversary of the end of the Second World War in Europe, May 16, 1995).

As an ecumenical confrontation (although in this instance the words of the Pope are more frank and precise than those of any other confessional organism) this is an admission of fault that is subscribed to by all the churches of Europe and it is contained in the final document published by the ecumenical assembly on Justice and Peace, held at Basle, Switzerland, on May 20, 1989: "We have caused conflicts and we have not been able to make use of all the opportunities for dialogue and reconciliation; we have tolerated and even too readily we have justified wars."

EIGHT

Religious Wars

The text that treats of religious wars is among the most beautiful of all Pope John Paul's requests for forgiveness. In fact, it is from this text that we selected the name for this book, *When a Pope Asks Forgiveness*. The very selection of the words indicates the intention of formulating a lapidary text: "Today I, the Pope of the Church of Rome, in the name of all Catholics, ask for forgiveness for the wounds inflicted on non-Catholics in the course of the troubled history of these peoples." The Pope made this statement in his homily for the canonization of Jan Sarkander (1576-1620) on May 21, 1995, at Olomouc in the Czech Republic. To this text we can add two others; the first, pronounced a month later in Slovakia and another that had been delivered six years previously at Salzburg. This is further proof that in the history of papal requests for forgiveness, each word has its mother and each gesture has its progenitor.

Asking and Giving Pardon

Below we cite a passage from the homily preached by Pope John Paul during the canonization of Jan

Sarkander at Olomouc in the Czech Republic. In it the Pope confronts the not unreasonable stiffening of the Lutheran Church (which felt that it was being accused in the canonization of a martyr who was condemned to death by the Protestant authorities). It shows that even in the field of ecumenism if a pope does not fear for himself, he can change iron into gold:

> Almost four centuries later we meet Jan Sarkander, priest and martyr. He is your special boast, dear Moravians. You have always loved and venerated him as your protector, particularly in the most painful moments of your history....
>
> This canonization must in no way reopen painful wounds, which in the past marked the Body of Christ in these lands. On the contrary, today I, the Pope of the Church of Rome, in the name of all Catholics, ask forgiveness for the wrongs inflicted on non-Catholics during the turbulent history of these peoples; at the same time, I pledge the Catholic Church's forgiveness for whatever harm her sons and daughters suffered. May this day mark a new beginning in the common effort to follow Christ, his Gospel, his law of love, his supreme desire for the unity of those who believe in him: "That they may all be one" (Jn 17:21) (At the canonization of Jan Sarkander, Olomouc, Czech Republic, May 21, 1995).

Homage to the Lutheran Martyrs

This request for forgiveness triggered another important revision of history as regards wars of religion. It was expressed a month and a half later, during a visit to Slovakia, on the occasion of the beatification of three martyrs who were put to death by the Protestant authorities at Kosice, Slovakia, in 1619:

> Today's liturgy invites us to reflect on the tragic events of the early 17th century, emphasizing, on the one

hand, the senselessness of violence relentlessly visited upon innocent victims and, on the other, the splendid example of so many followers of Christ who were able to face sufferings of every kind without going against their own consciences. Besides the three martyrs of Kosice, many other people, also belonging to other Christian confessions, were subjected to torture and suffered heavy punishment; some were even put to death. How can we fail to acknowledge, for example, the spiritual greatness of the twenty-four members of the Evangelical Churches who were killed at Presov? To them and to all who accepted suffering and death out of fidelity to the dictates of their conscience the Church gives praise and expresses admiration (Homily at the beatification of three martyrs, Kosice, Slovakia, July 2, 1995).

To recognize the "spiritual greatness" of twenty-four Evangelical Protestants put to death by Catholics is perhaps a great deal more than to ask forgiveness for "the wounds inflicted by Catholics on non-Catholics." It is a gesture *ad extra* when compared to the sentiment *ad intra* which is expressed in the beatification ceremony. It really completes the request for forgiveness that was expressed at Olomouc. Both the one and the other have been crowned by a genial and unexpected act by the Pope, namely, his act of homage at the monument dedicated to the Lutheran martyrs on the afternoon of July 2 at Presov.

There is John Paul II, walking in the rain and in silence toward a corner of the city square in the ancient city of Presov. He stands before the monument honoring the Calvinist martyrs who were killed by Catholics in 1687. It is one of the most humble and striking ecumenical gestures ever performed by this Pontiff. And it had not been scheduled; it was a last-minute decision.

The Pope prayed silently in front of the monument, perhaps asking forgiveness from those poor Christians who died for their faith because they refused to submit to the papacy and were killed by other Christians who were defending the papacy.

The Lutheran Bishop of Presov, Jan Midriak, was in attendance, and after the silent prayer, he greeted the Pope and thanked him for having made the visit. Then together they recited the Our Father. Later, Bishop Midriak told the journalists: "We are truly grateful for this gesture; we never thought that anything like this would ever happen." And when the Pope returned to Rome, he also recalled the visit at a general audience:

> This canonization was also an important ecumenical event, as was evident both at my meeting with representatives of the Protestant denominations and during my visit to the place that commemorates the death of a group of the faithful of the Reformation, condemned in the 17th century in the name of the principle *"cuius regio eius religio."* A monument erected in the city of Presov recalls the event. I paused to pray before it (General Audience, July 5, 1995).

The Unjust Expulsion of Protestants

The third text is the oldest and the least explicit, but like the other two, it acknowledges the resentment that was felt on both sides by the adversaries in the religious wars. It contains implicitly what is explicit in the other two pronouncements; in fact it anticipates them in their essential points.

These words were spoken by Pope John Paul II at Salzburg during an ecumenical ceremony with the Evangelical community. Salzburg did not suffer any religious wars, thanks to the diplomatic gestures of Archbishop Paride Lodron (1619-1653). But Salzburg did suffer a delayed blow a century later, when Archbishop Leopold Firmian expelled 30,000 Protestants (about 15% of the population) in 1731 because they refused to take part in the missions that were organized periodically for their conversion. On this wound, 250 years later, Pope John Paul poured the soothing oil of his words (1988):

> Here at Salzburg we also find the Reformation. We are prompted to recall the unjust expulsion of Protestants from this place in the 18th and 19th centuries, in accordance with the principle *"cuius regio eius religio,"* which was legally applicable in former times. But many years ago the Archbishop of Salzburg asked pardon of our Evangelical brothers and sisters in the name of the whole archdiocese for the injustice they suffered. The fact that today we listen to the word of God together and pray for one another in an Evangelical church is a clear sign that this prayer for forgiveness has been accepted and has led to reconciliation (A meeting with the Evangelical community, Salzburg, Austria, June 26, 1988).

The scandals of the religious wars have pushed Europe toward atheism. And therefore the impulse of the Church to make amends should be proportionate to their negative effect. This is the way Father Georges Cottier speaks of it:

> Some Christians, especially in certain centuries, have consented to the use of intolerance and even of violence with the intention of serving truth. We know that in the genesis of modern unbelief, the sentiments of mutual hostility which divided Christians felt for each other during the period of religious wars had a great deal of influence. They were a scandal to souls who had not yet lost the sense of moderation and respect toward

their neighbor. How was it possible to defend the truth of the Gospel with methods that are fundamentally opposed to the evangelical spirit? The intrinsic bond, which some wanted to see between the spirit of tolerance and agnosticism regarding basic principles, has been instead a pitiful response to the fanaticism of religious struggles.[44]

NINE

Hus, Calvin and Zwingli

A "faithful reading of the facts" compels a rewriting of history and the recognition of the "spiritual greatness" of former adversaries. We saw this in our discussion on religious wars and we shall see it again when we speak of Martin Luther, the most calumniated of all the opponents of the Church but the one who, up until the present time, has been treated more justly. Pope John Paul has invited us to look with new eyes on some ancient opponents and he has selected three reformers for special attention: Hus, Calvin and Zwingli. He spoke of them during his visits to the lands in which they were protagonists of the Reformation, where they are still followed by the communities which they founded.

Jan Hus

During his visit to the former Czechoslovakia in April, 1990, Pope John Paul revised the judgment on the Reformer, Jan Hus, a Bohemian who was excommunicated in 1411, condemned to death by the Council of Constance and burned at the stake in 1415. In his revision of history, the Pope referred to an intervention by Cardinal Beran at the Second Vatican Council, thus indicating one of the men who had inspired his project of revising history in the light of the Gospel:

> I recall that at the Second Vatican Council the Czech Archbishop, Cardinal Josef Beran, made a forceful statement in defence of the principles of religious freedom and tolerance, referring with heartbreaking words to the case of the Bohemian priest Jan Hus and deploring the excesses to which people abandoned themselves both then and thereafter. I still recall those words of the Cardinal Archbishop of Prague regarding this priest, who played such an important role in the religious and cultural history of the Bohemian people. It will be the task of experts—in the first place Czech theologians—to define more precisely the place which John Hus occupies among the reformers of the Church, besides the other famous reforming figures of the Bohemian Middle Ages, such as Thomas of Stitne and John Milic of Kromeriz. Nevertheless, over and above the theological convictions which he championed, Hus cannot be denied personal integrity of life and a commitment to the instruction and moral education of the nation (Meeting with the world of culture, Prague, April 21, 1990).

Cardinal Beran's intervention at the Second Vatican Council during the debate on the document, *Declaration on Religious Freedom* (September 20, 1965), was extraordinary:

> Everywhere and always, the violation of freedom of conscience gives birth to hypocrisy. And one can say that hypocrisy in practicing the faith is more harmful to the Church than the hypocrisy of concealing it, which is very common in our day.
>
> So, in my country, the Catholic Church at this time seems to be making painful amends for mistakes and

sins committed in times gone by in her name against freedom of conscience, such as the 15th century burning of the priest Jan Hus and during the 17th century the forced reconversion of a great part of the Czech people to the Catholic faith under the motto *"cuius regio eius religio"* ("the people of a territory follow the religion of its ruler").

By such acts, the secular arm, wishing or pretending to serve the Catholic Church, in reality left a deep wound in the hearts of the people. This trauma created a huge obstacle to progress in their spiritual life, offering the enemies of the Church, even today, excuses for attacking her.

Thus even history admonishes us to enunciate in this Council, clearly and without any restrictions otherwise it would smack of opportunism—the principle of religious liberty and freedom of conscience. If this is done, and additionally in a spirit of penance for sins committed in the past in this area, the moral authority of our Church will be held in great esteem and this will redound to the benefit of the world.[45]

As a matter of fact, the name of Hus, together with the names of Savonarola and Bartolomeo de Las Casas, were turned over to the historico-theological commission by Pope John Paul in order to prepare for the examination of conscience at the end of the present millennium that would lead to a confession of faults and a request for forgiveness. We have already seen that the commission decided to abandon the study of individual historical personages and to focus on two principal questions: anti-Semitism and the Inquisitions. Perhaps it is right that particular cases, especially those that are of relevance to local regions, should not be handled by a central organism; it would seem to be more logical to leave them in the hands of national ecclesiastical communities.

The fact is that both Catholic and Evangelical communities in Bohemia are working on the case of Hus. Cardinal Miloslav Vlk, Archbishop of Prague, announced: "We have set up an ecumenical commission to investigate the person and life of Jan Hus. We have created a basis of collaboration and exchange that is, I would say, a model, because there is truly a very fraternal atmosphere."[46]

This project has already produced some fruit. On July 6, 1995, Cardinal Vlk participated in a commemoration of Jan Hus, held at the church in which Hus began preaching on reform in 1400. It was the first time that a representative of the Catholic Church took part in such an event. This "first time" was a favorite reference in the ecumenical pronouncements and the gestures of reconciliation by Pope John Paul during his visits to the Czech Republic and Slovakia.

Calvin and Zwingli

Regarding the two Swiss reformers, Pope Wojtyla spoke of them during his visit to Switzerland in June of 1984. At an ecumenical meeting he acknowledged that the intention of Calvin and Zwingli was "to make the Church more faithful to the will of the Lord":

> This year the memory of the zeal which animated two outstanding religious personalities in Swiss history is present in our mind: the first is Huldrych Zwingli, whose five hundredth anniversary you are celebrating by various public events honoring his person and his work; the second is John Calvin, who was born four hundred and seventy-five years ago.
>
> We find the historical influence of their witness not only in the area of theology and ecclesial structure, but also in the cultural, social and political fields. The

legacy of the thought and ethical convictions particular to each of these two men continues to be forcefully and dynamically present in various parts of Christianity. On the one hand, we cannot forget that the work of their reform remains a permanent challenge among us and makes our ecclesial divisions always present; but, on the other hand, no one can deny that elements in the theology and spirituality of each one of them maintain deep ties between us.

The fact that we judge in a different manner the complex events of the history of that time as well as the differences which persist in central questions of our faith must not divide us forever. Above all, the memory of the events of the past must not limit the liberty of our present efforts to repair the damage caused by those events. The cleansing of our memories is an element of capital importance in ecumenical progress.It implies the frank acknowledgment of reciprocal wrongs and errors committed in the way of reacting toward each other when indeed each one wanted to make the Church more faithful to the will of the Lord.

Perhaps the day will come, and I hope it will be soon, when Swiss Catholics and Protestants will be able to write the history of that troubled and complex period together, with an objectivity rooted in deep fraternal charity. Such an achievement will allow us to commit the past to the mercy of God without reserve and to reach out, in complete freedom, to the future to make it more in keeping with his will (cf. Phil 3:13), who wills that all his holy people have but one heart and one mind (cf. Acts 4:24) in order to unite in the praise and the proclamation of the glory of his grace (cf. Eph 1:6) (Meeting with the Federation of Protestant Churches, Kehrsatz, Switzerland, June 14, 1984).

TEN

The Indians

Pope John Paul has done much more for the Indians than has been reported. More than forty times he has met with the Indians of America and the natives of every continent. Five times he has acknowledged the historical injustices done to them by Christians.

On one occasion the Pope said that those Christians "were unable to see the Indians as their brothers." It was October 13, 1992, the fifth centenary of the discovery of America, and the Holy Father had gone to Santo Domingo to celebrate the beginning of the evangelization of those people. He also said on that occasion that it is necessary to make a confession of the sins of the past five centuries. When he returned to Rome, he described his trip as an "act of atonement," and this was his second comment about the confession of sins, more emphatic than the first one.

The third, fourth and fifth references were earlier than 1992; they were less solemn but more precise in pointing out the responsibility of Christians and the Church. One of the statements was made in Canada in

1984, and it was a reference to the mistakes and damage caused by the missionaries. Another statement was made in 1986, and it was addressed to the aborigines of Australia. The Pope acknowledged how long it took even Christians of good will in our day to admit the oppression that took place yesterday and to a great extent still continues today. The last statement occurred in 1987 at a meeting with North American Indians in Phoenix, Arizona. The Pope admitted that there were members of the Church among those who were guilty of "cultural oppression" and the "destruction" of the Indians' way of life.

Enormous Suffering

This is the first of the texts that referred to Indians of Latin America:

> How could the Church, which has always been close to indigenous peoples, through her religious, priests and bishops, forget in this fifth centenary the enormous sufferings inflicted on the inhabitants of this continent during the period of the conquest and colonization? It is necessary to acknowledge in all sincerity the abuses committed due to the lack of love on the part of those persons who were unable to see the natives as their brothers, as children of the same Father (Message to the Indians, Santo Domingo, October 13, 1992).

An Act of Atonement

On his return to Rome, Pope John Paul spoke about his "act of atonement," and it is perhaps the only place in which he spoke so clearly about it:

> Through my pilgrimage to the place where evangelization began, a pilgrimage characterized by thanksgiving,

we wanted at the same time to make an act of atonement before the infinite holiness of God for everything which during that advance toward the American continent was marred by sin, injustice and violence. Some of the missionaries have left us an impressive witness. One need only recall the names of Montesinos, Las Casas, Cârdoba, Juan del Valle and many others.

After five hundred years we stand before Christ, who is the Lord of all human history, to address those words to the Father that Christ himself taught us: "Forgive us our trespasses as we forgive..." (cf. Mt 6:12). The Redeemer's prayer is addressed to the Father and at the same time to all who suffered various injustices.

We do not cease asking these people for "forgiveness." This request for pardon is primarily addressed to the first inhabitants of the new land, the Indians, and then to those who were brought from Africa as slaves to do heavy labor.

"Forgive us our trespasses." This prayer is also part of evangelization (General Audience, St. Peter's, Rome, October 21, 1992).

Faults of the Missionaries

The Pope made a rare reference to the historical responsibility of missionaries when he addressed native Indians in Canada eight years earlier. His statements amounted to a formal correction of the teaching of the past and a challenge to the present:

It is clear from the historical record that over the centuries your peoples have been repeatedly the victims of injustice by newcomers who, in their blindness, often saw your culture as inferior.... It is time for forgiveness, for reconciliation and for a commitment to building new relationships.... And so today, in speaking to you, I present to you the Gospel message with its commandment of fraternal love, with its demands for justice and

for human rights and with all its liberating power....
Today I want to proclaim that freedom which is required
for a just and equitable measure of self-determination
in your own lives as native peoples. In union with the
whole Church I proclaim all your rights—and their cor-
responding duties. And I also condemn physical, cultural and religious oppression, and all that would in any
way deprive you or any group of what rightly belongs to
you (Address to Innuit Indians, Yellow Knife, Canada,
September 18, 1984).

A few days before this meeting, the Holy Father had
said to another group of Indians:

Your encounter with the Gospel has not only enriched
you, it has enriched the Church. We are well aware that
this has not taken place without its difficulties and, occasionally, its serious mistakes (Meeting with the natives,
Ste. Anne de Beaupré, Canada, September 10, 1984).

The acknowledgment of the faults committed by
missionaries is really an echo of what the Apostolic Delegate to the United States, Archbishop Pio Laghi, had
said at the "Tekakwitha Conference" in September,
1983, to the delegates of the Indian population of North
America: "In preaching Christianity, many missionaries
have voiced the conviction that the cultural institutions
of the natives are inferior to those of the white man.
For this we not only express our regret but we ask your
forgiveness."

Grieving Christians

The message that Pope Wojtyla gave to the Aborigines of Australia in November, 1986, brought the denunciation up to date as regards the insensibility of so many
Christians to the drama of the natives:

Christian people of good will are saddened to realize—
many of them only recently—for how long a time Ab-
original people were transported from their home-
lands into small areas or reserves where families were
broken up, tribes split apart, children orphaned and
people forced to live like exiles in a foreign country
(Address to the Aborigines, Alica Springs, Australia,
November 29, 1986).

Learning from the Errors of the Past

With the following text we are in the United States,
where perhaps the insensibility to the sufferings of the
North American Indians has been more pervasive and
the responsibility of Catholics has been less acknowledged. But by this time the Pope is not making such
distinctions. When he speaks of the responsibility of
Christians, he means all Christians. He is willing to take
on the blame for the sins of those who do not even consider him as their representative:

The early encounter between your traditional cultures
and the European way of life was an event of such significance and change that it profoundly affects your
collective life even today. That encounter was a harsh
and painful reality for your peoples. The cultural oppression, the injustices, the disruption of your life and
of your traditional societies must be acknowledged....
Unfortunately, not all the members of the Church lived
up to their Christian responsibilities. But let us not
dwell excessively on mistakes and wrongs, even as we
commit ourselves to overcoming their present effects....
Now, we are called to learn from the mistakes of the
past and we must work together for reconciliation and
healing, as brothers and sisters in Christ (Phoenix, Arizona, September 14, 1987).

The mea culpa which the Pope addressed to the Indians and Aborigines is very generous. Nevertheless,
the confession of sin is still one of the most controversial
questions in the Catholic Church. When the Pope acknowledges the mistakes of the missionaries, there are
missionaries of good faith who resent it. And if he
speaks of the faults in general of Christians in a particular region, referring to some of the members of the
episcopacy, to groups of radicals in the Church, or to
traditional anti-clericals, he will perhaps offend the majority and the more devout members. So he sees that it
is necessary to correct or balance the self-criticism with a
vindication of all the good that has been done.

Here is a very evident example of a similar apologetic retrospect in regard to the Indians. It is a discourse
to a group of Brazilian bishops who had come to Rome
for their *ad limina* visit. It took place three years after
the Pope's visit to Santo Domingo and it seems to indi-
cate that many among the bishops had not been in
agreement with him:

> Of course, as you well know, there has been no lack of
> shadows: choices and attitudes which are still deplor-
> able, even when taking into account the different
> philosophical and cultural concepts of the age. Never-
> theless, this must not be a reason to scorn the extraor-
> dinary results achieved by countless pioneers who,
> making huge sacrifices, contributed to spreading the
> seed of the Gospel throughout the country....
>
> The Church looks back with serenity, since she ful-
> filled her duty, despite the difficulties that such an
> evangelization had to overcome in the historical and
> social context.
>
> With regard to the indigenous peoples, the Church
> did not cease to raise her clear, firm voice in the words
> of my Predecessor Paul III, who vehemently con-
> demned the attempts to enslave them (cf. *Sublimis*

Deus, 1537). Despite the obstacle of the cultural environment, the human dignity and consequent rights of the Indian were recognized in the Church's practice and discipline. The experience of faith resulting from the foundation of the missions was significant in that it recognized and took up all the more positive aspects of indigenous culture, promoting their capabilities, arts and occupations, pedagogically leading the Indians to a knowledge of revealed Truth and defending them from those who wished to exploit them.

Today we cannot but admire the pastoral sensitivity of the early missionaries who sympathetically accepted the noblest traits they found in that cultural context, such as the sacred character attributed to creation, respect for Mother Nature and integration with her, the community spirit of solidarity between generations, the balance between work and rest, loyalty and love of freedom. They enhanced all this with explicit Gospel teaching, integrating it and sublimating it into the Christian heritage. These heralds of the Gospel thus achieved a living and original synthesis by fostering an authentic inculturation of the faith (Meeting with a group of bishops from Brazil, St. Peter's, April 1, 1995).

Possibly the Pope will again take up the question of native peoples and thus complete his revision of history. The United Nations has already called for a ten-year period dedicated internationally to indigenous populations (December 1994 to December 2004), which includes the year 2000. Moreover, it is known that the Pope pays very close attention to the programs of the United Nations. It is our impression that he has given much thought to this topic, but as yet not as much as he could.

As we have previously noted, the non-Catholic churches are very competent at self-examination and admission of fault, even in regard to indigenous peoples.

An example of this can be found in the final document issued by the International Ecumenical Assembly held at Seoul, March 5 to 12, 1990. It called on all the world-wide members to mark the five hundredth anniversary of the invasion of the Americas, not as an occasion for exaltation but for confession, reparation and repentance because of the brutal genocide and exploitation of native peoples.

Within the Catholic Church there have been and there still are some voices raised in radical self-criticism of the colonization and evangelization of Latin America. Pope John Paul II has not and perhaps cannot agree with them, but he has at least taken notice of them. It suffices to record the statement made by Bishop Leonidas Proano of Riobamba, Ecuador, on his deathbed in 1988: "Suddenly the thought comes to me, the fixed idea that the Church is the sole entity responsible for this heavy weight with which the Indians have been burdened for centuries. How sad, how sad! I bear on my shoulders this centuries-old burden."[47]

Perhaps one day a mestizo pope will go beyond the request for pardon expressed by Pope Wojtyla and will say something that will take into account the last testament of Bishop Leonidas.

ELEVEN

Injustices

This particular chapter is incomplete because it deals with the vast area of injustices for which Christians and the Church are responsible, but thus far Pope John Paul has said little about it. As he did when treating of dictators, he has written the title and has stated the fundamental thesis, but he has not yet developed it in any great detail. For example, this is the way he referred to injustices in his Apostolic Letter for the Great Jubilee:

> And should we not also regret, among the shadows of our own day, the responsibility shared by so many Christians for grave forms of injustice and exclusion? It must be asked how many Christians really know and put into practice the principles of the Church's social doctrine (*Tertio Millennio Adveniente*, 36).

The co-responsibility for injustices to which the Pope refers here had already been emphasized two years earlier as "sins against charity":

> We must recognize the fact that, since the Church is a community which is also composed of sinners, the precept of love has at times been transgressed over the centuries. It is a question of failures on the part of in-

dividuals and groups who bear the name Christian, failures on the level of reciprocal relations, both inter-personal as well as social and international. It is a sad reality which appears in the history of individuals and nations, and also in the Church's history. Conscious of their own vocation to love according to Christ's ex-ample, Christians confess these sins against love with humility and repentance, without, however, ceasing to believe in love, which St. Paul says, "bears all things" and "never fails" (1 Cor 13:7-8). But if the history of humanity and of the Church herself abounds in sins against charity, which cause sadness and pain, we must at the same time acknowledge with joy and gratitude that in every Christian age there have been marvelous acts of witness which confirm love; and that many times—as we have noted—this testimony has been he-roic (General Audience, St. Peter's, June 3, 1992).

Co-responsibility for injustices and sins against charity are mentioned as sinful actions, but the Pope also makes reference to the sin of omission, which is the failure to denounce injustices. Pope John Paul indicated this in his address to youth at Strasbourg in 1988:

The earth belongs to God, but it has been given to all human beings. It is not God's will that some waste while others go hungry; that some have abundance be-cause their soil is fertile, while others are destitute be-cause they do not have this good fortune. It should not be that the rich and the strong enjoy privileges while injustice is reserved for the poor and the disabled....

Does the Church assert this strongly enough? Per-haps not. The members of the Church have their weak-nesses as well. We are the Church, you and I (Meeting with youth, Strasbourg, October 8, 1988).

It has been said of Pope Wojtyla that he willingly ad-mits the sins of Christians but never the sins of the

Church. But in the preceding quotation he explicitly names the Church. Three years earlier, addressing the European Economic Community at Brussels, he also admitted the responsibility of Christians for international sins of injustice and for sins during the period of colonialism:

> However, our predecessors also opened new ways toward other inhabited lands. Prompted by the desire to know this world entrusted to man and having technically progressed, they go off to discover continents new to them. Surprising adventures! They go to plant the cross, to share Christian hope, to diffuse their intellectual and technical progress. But at the same time they are conquerors, they want to impose their culture, they appropriate the riches of other ethnic groups whose traditions they often disdain and whom they too often cruelly subject to their power (Visit to the European Economic Community, Brussels, May 20, 1985).

We can also quote another passage, and perhaps a more important one, in which the Pope refers to the wealth of the churches, but without enlarging on it. The passage is contained in the Encyclical *Sollicitudo Rei Socialis* (1988), which calls for justice and emphasizes "the duty of the Church to alleviate the misery of those who suffer want not only in regard to superfluous things but also in regard to the necessities of life":

> Thus, part of the teaching and most ancient practice of the Church is her conviction that she is obliged by her vocation—she herself, her ministers and each of her members—to relieve the misery of the suffering, both far and near, not only out of her "abundance" but also out of her "necessities." Faced by cases of need, one cannot ignore them in favor of superfluous church ornaments and costly furnishings for divine worship; on

the contrary, it should be obligatory to sell these goods in order to provide food, drink, clothing and shelter for those who lack these things.... I wish to insist once more on the seriousness and urgency of that teaching, and I ask the Lord to give all Christians the strength to put it faithfully into practice (*Sollicitudo Rei Socialis,* 31).

The invitation to the churches to sell their gold in order to provide bread for the poor contains an implicit but strong self-criticism of the preferences and priorities of the past, when wealth was accumulated and hunger was even greater. This is an overriding theme which Pope Wojtyla will leave to his successor: while the churches of the Old World, which are rich in treasures, are becoming empty, and the poor ecclesial communities of the southern hemisphere are flourishing, the sale of those treasures in order to help the poor may soon become obligatory. Already in February of 1976, when he was Patriarch of Venice, Albino Luciani, who later became Pope John Paul I for a month, had invited his parish priests to hold such a sale. Perhaps this will be done in cathedrals throughout the world with the beginning of the third millennium.

A request for forgiveness for the abuses against justice, often connected with every other kind of sin, is contained in a prayer approved by Pope John Paul II for the celebration of the closing of the European Synod in 1991:

O Lord, our Reconciler, in the Christian communities of Europe our divisions, our egoism and the scandals of those who say they belong to Christ but lack the power and authority to work for peace, justice and liberty, have weakened in the conscience of the people their faith in the new life which you have brought. Pardon us and have pity on us (Ecumenical celebration, St. Peter's, December 7, 1991).

Up to this time we have not found any other text of the Pope that should be quoted in this chapter. It is necessary to wait for a more explicit word that may be forthcoming tomorrow. And it is only logical to expect something further from a Polish Christian who has suffered injustice, from a priest who has been a laborer, and from a pope who has so often declared (e.g., in Medellin, Colombia, July 6, 1986) that "no one can snatch from the hands of the Church the banner of justice."

It can be said that the Pope has looked upon all of his preaching as "a truly Christian provocation for those who possess and control the earth" (spoken in the Philippines in 1981). And the Holy Father has continued to exhort the bishops of the Third World to "denounce all violations of justice as actions contrary to the Gospel" (Bolivia, 1988). He also reminded the Christians of the northern hemisphere of God's judgment: "the poor South will judge the wealthy North" (Edmonton, Canada, September, 1984). All that remains is the application of these papal statements to the works of charity and justice, indicating times and places, as he has done in other areas.

If some people think that the Pope has really said very little, the fact is that no one has said much more. Thus, on November 25, 1985, after making his presentation to the Extraordinary Synod in Rome, Cardinal Daneels told reporters: "We have not always been faithful to our duty toward the poor and to the preferential option for the poor." The secretary general of CELAM, Archbishop Castrillon Hoyos spoke in the same tone at a news conference during that same Extraordinary Synod: "Since Medellin, the Church is trying to eliminate the causes of the scandalous phenomenon of great injustices that are found in a continent that is traditionally Catholic." And Cardinal Lorscheider of Brazil was the only one to speak with great passion in the Synod itself, challenging the entire Church to "a genuine conversion of mind, life and practice" in order to have direct contact with the poor and to do so with "an attitude of listening, humility and surrender of possessions."

The examination of conscience on social questions is also very weak in the field of ecumenism. Nevertheless, in the final Ecumenical Assembly of the churches of Europe, held at Basle, Switzerland, under the title "Justice and Peace," we find this statement: "In the great social conflicts, in which the cry for justice could be heard, the churches remained silent" (May 20, 1989). Similarly, at the close of the Worldwide Assembly of Churches, held in Seoul, Korea, we find a similar declaration: "The churches admit that they need to be freed from their complicity with unjust social systems.... We admit with sorrow that we, as churches, have not been in the first line of the defense of human rights and that many times we have used our theology to justify violations of human rights" (1990).

It is easy to preach justice, but it is difficult to admit one's own injustice. It is time for an examination of conscience. I once asked the Superior General of the Jesuits, Peter Hans Kolvenbach, what he thought of the Pope's invitation to a confession of mea culpa. He responded: "I find the proposal to be a good one, especially in regard to the errors that are still having bad effects, such as those that led to the division of the churches and those against the poor. We have not always come to the defense of the latter nor have social injustices always been combatted." And here is the point: "the transgressions against the poor" (i.e. sins against charity and justice) still exist and they are what muffle the voice of the churches.

TWELVE

The Inquisition

Pope Wojtyla has spoken three times about the "errors" of the Inquisition, and once he referred to the methods of "intolerance and even of violence" that were used. He approved the listing of the Inquisition, together with anti-Semitism, as the principal topics for the examination of conscience at the end of the second millennium. These two topics will be treated in one of the two international congresses to be held by the historico-theological commission in 1999, as we have already mentioned.

Intolerance and Violence

We begin with the Pope's reference to the methods of "intolerance and even of violence" which the Holy Father mentioned in his Apostolic Letter announcing the Great Jubilee:

> Another painful chapter of history to which the sons and daughters of the Church must return with a spirit of repentance is that of the acquiescence given, especially in certain centuries, to intolerance and even to the use of violence in the service of truth.

It is true that an accurate historical judgment cannot prescind from careful study of the cultural conditioning of the times, as a result of which many people may have held in good faith that an authentic witness to the truth could include suppressing the opinion of others or at least paying no attention to them. Many factors frequently converged to create assumptions which justified intolerance and fostered an emotional climate from which only great spirits, truly free and filled with God, were in some way able to break free. Yet the consideration of mitigating factors does not exonerate the Church from the obligation to express profound regret for the weaknesses of so many of her sons and daughters who sullied her face, preventing her from fully mirroring the image of her crucified Lord, the supreme exemplar of patient love and of humble meekness. From these painful moments of the past a lesson can be drawn for the future, leading all Christians to adhere fully to the sublime principle stated by the Council: "The truth cannot impose itself except by virtue of its own truth, as it wins over the mind with both gentleness and power" (*Tertio Millennio Adveniente,* 35).

Errors and Excesses

The first time that Pope Wojtyla explicitly spoke of the errors of the Inquisition was during his first visit to Spain in 1982:

If in certain moments such as those of the Inquisition there were tensions, errors and excesses—facts which the Church today can consider in the objective light of history—it is necessary to acknowledge that the Spanish intellectual climate of the time was such that they were able to reconcile in an amazing way the demands of complete freedom of research with a profound sense of the Church (Meeting with the academic and scientific world of the university, Madrid, November 3, 1982).

This brief reference is no small thing, even though it strikes an apologetic note, because it breaks a long-standing taboo. It had never happened before, not even in the days of the evangelical Roncalli or the reformer Montini, that a pope would refer to the Inquisition in an unfavorable light. Until the reform of the Curia by Pope Pius X in 1908, the very word "Inquisition" was held in such honor that it became part of the official title of the Congregation of the Holy Office, which was designated as "The Sacred Congregation of the Roman and Universal Inquisition."

To break a taboo does not always mean to zero in on an argument which up to that moment the taboo had prevented one from discussing. The first occasion on which the Pope did so, six years later, he did not specifically name the Inquisition, but he did describe precisely the questions that it dealt with and the problem that it posed in the historical memory of Christians, namely, the question of the primacy of conscience, which had been violated by that tribunal:

> The Church affirms that there is in man an indomitable awareness of the conditions that affect him, a consciousness capable of recognizing his true dignity and being open to the absolute, a consciousness that is the source of fundamental choices guided by the search for good for others as well as for self, a consciousness that is the place of a responsible freedom. It is true that there has been a lot of drifting away, and Christians know that they have played a part in it (Address to the Parliamentary Assembly of Europe, Strasbourg, October 8, 1988).

Violence in the Name of the Faith

Here is the third text in which the Pope speaks of the Inquisition, It is contained in the memorandum which he sent to the cardinals early in 1994 for the Extraordinary Consistory, which was to prepare for the Great Jubilee:

> How can we remain silent in the face of so many forms of violence perpetrated in the name of the faith? Religious wars, the courts of the Inquisition and other forms of violation of the rights of individuals.... It is significant that the coercive methods, injurious to human rights, were later employed by the totalitarian ideologies of the twentieth century and are now being used by the Islamic fundamentalists. From those kinds of coercive methods came the crimes of Hitler's Nazism and Marxist Stalinism. A correct reaction to all of this is the *Declaration of the Rights of Man* and, in the Church, the *Declaration on Religious Liberty* issued by Vatican Council II. It is also necessary, in the light of what the Vatican Council has said, that the Church, on its own initiative, should look again at the dark aspects of its own history, judging it in the light of the principles of the Gospel (From the memorandum sent to the cardinals, Spring, 1994).

This is perhaps the text in which Pope John Paul II most clearly focuses on the Inquisition as a topic for examination at the end of the second millennium. It concentrates on the use of violence in the name and service of the faith, rather than the errors and excesses which were used to justify such violence. As we already demonstrated, Pope John Paul had previously spoken of the errors and excesses in a somewhat defensive vein when he visited Spain in 1982. Twelve years later, the tone is no longer defensive and the question is not about errors and excesses, but the very existence of the Inquisition. Consequently, the arguments of those who insist that the Inquisition was more moderate and more just than other tribunals in the Middle Ages are completely out of place. The Pope is not raising a question about the methods used by the Inquisition, but of the very existence of the Inquisition. Hence, he links it to every other form of "violence in the name of the faith." For a more complete picture, one should read this Chapter together with the Chapters on the Crusades, Religious Wars and Integralism.

THIRTEEN

Integralism

When he uses the word "integralism," what does Pope John Paul mean and what does he condemn? He is speaking of "religious integralism" and he says that it was in error yesterday and is unacceptable today. He speaks of it in only one text, but it is extraordinarily clear, a real milestone in the Roman pontificate. The passage is contained in an allocution given at Strasbourg before the European Parliament in 1988:

> According to some people, civil and political freedom, already won by the overturning of the old order based on religious faith, is still understood as going hand in hand with the marginalization, indeed the suppression, of religion, in which they tend to see a system of alienation. For some believers, on the other hand, a life of faith is not possible without a return to that old order, which they frequently idealize. These two opposing attitudes do not contain any solution that would be compatible with the Christian message and the spirit of Europe. For, where civil freedom reigns and religious liberty is fully guaranteed, faith can only grow in strength by facing the challenge posed by unbelief, and atheism cannot but see its own limitations in the challenge which faith gives it.

Faced with this diversity of points of view, the highest function of the law is to guarantee to all citizens equally the right to live in accordance with their consciences and not to contradict the norms of the natural moral order which are recognized by reason.

At this point, it seems important to me to mention that it was from the soil of Christianity that modern Europe took the principle—often lost sight of during the centuries of "Christendom"—that most fundamentally governs its public life: I mean the principle, proclaimed for the first time by Christ, of the distinction between "what is Caesar's" and "what is God's" (cf. Mt 22:21). This essential distinction between the arranging of the external framework of the earthly city and the autonomy of the person becomes clear in light of the respective natures of the political community, to which all citizens necessarily belong, and that of the religious community, to which believers freely adhere....

Our European history clearly shows how often the dividing line between "what is Caesar's" and "what is God's" has been crossed in both directions. Medieval Latin Christendom, to mention only one example, while theoretically elaborating the natural concept of the State, taking up the great tradition of Aristotle, did not always avoid the integralist temptation of excluding from the temporal community those who did not profess the true faith. Religious integralism, which makes no distinction between the proper spheres of faith and civil life, which is still practiced in other parts of the world, seems to be incompatible with the very spirit of Europe, as it has been shaped by the Christian message (Visit to the Parliament of Europe, Strasbourg, October 11, 1988).

There are four essential affirmations in this self-examination concerning integralism (which may also be understood as "extreme religious chauvinism or fundamentalism" [tr. note]):

1. Understood as a tendency to exclude from the civil community anyone who does not profess the true faith, it is incompatible with the Christian distinction between that which belongs to God and that which belongs to Caesar;

2. Medieval Christianity lost sight of this distinction and therefore could not overcome the temptation to apply an integralist exclusion;

3. Today there are some believers who would like to restore that ancient system, without taking into account that they are preserving an attitude that would lead to a practice that is incompatible with the Christian message;

4. In the civil context, religious integralism is also incompatible with the spirit of Europe, which is characterized by the Christian teaching, as distinct, for example, from Islamic integralism and atheistic integralism.

The text that we have quoted is a pivotal text in the pontificate of Pope John Paul. What Lamennais and Buonaiuti, Maritain and von Balthasar would have given to hear those words from the lips of a pope! They also tried to put the Church on guard against the danger of integralism, but they were condemned or censured for using that forbidden word. We shall now give some other quotations that illustrate the importance of the lengthy passage from the Pope's speech at Strasbourg.

This is how the Pope referred to the question early in 1996, when he spoke about the Council's *Declaration on Religious Freedom,* a freedom which is denied by those who follow religious integralism:

It is well known that as regards the question of relations among diverse cultures and religions, the attitudes of the various human communities, of states and sometimes of the believers themselves have not always been characterized by respect and tolerance. The Church, for her part, has experienced persecution from the very beginning of her history. On the other hand, even the Council has honestly acknowledged that among Christians also "from time to time there have been ways of acting that scarcely conform to the spirit of the Gospel, but are actually contrary to it" (Sunday message, St. Peter's, February 18, 1996).

The Holy Father had already admitted, in his message for the World Day of Peace (January 1, 1991), what "in the course of centuries" Christians have left to be desired in the area of religious tolerance:

As for religious intolerance, it cannot be denied that, despite the firm teaching of the Catholic Church according to which no one ought to be compelled to believe, throughout the centuries not a few misunderstandings and even conflicts have occurred between Christians and members of other religions. This fact was formally acknowledged by the Second Vatican Council, which stated that "in the life of the People of God as it has made its pilgrim way through the vicissitudes of human history, there have at times appeared ways of acting which were less in accord with the ways of the Gospel" (Message for the World Day of Peace, December 18, 1990).

The relationship between the cross and the sword also entered into the papal self-examination, when in Santo Domingo the Pope admitted "the truth with humility":

The Church does not deny the connection between the cross and the sword, which characterized the first phase of missionary activity in the New World (Address to the bishops of Latin America, Santo Domingo, October 12, 1984).

Father Georges Cottier, OP, theologian for the papal household, has analyzed the temptation of the medieval Church to integralism: "It has long been held that the quality of being a Christian consists in one's primary adherence to the political society within the ambit of the Christian State. As a means of defense, the State intervened in the religious domain with appropriate coercive measures. Along parallel lines, the Church made use of the temporal power. In this way a great number of interventions, under the label of intolerance and violence, were perpetrated by the State, which had become involved in spiritual matters in order to protect its integrity. As everyone knows, there have been tragic abuses that contaminated Christian history. The principle that was enforced at the end of the religious wars, *cuius regio eius religio,* is essentially a pagan principle."[48]

As a sign of the harmonious relationship between the Pope and his Dominican theologian we can point to the fact that the Holy Father has frequently made the same judgment as Father Cottier concerning the principle *cuius regio eius religio.* He did so during a general audience in July, 1995, as we have already noted, and in an address during an ecumenical meeting in Salzburg in September, 1983.

But someone could ask regarding the Pope, who condemned integralism, and his theologian, who explains it from a doctrinal point of view (and is there not a strange twist of history in assigning this role to a Dominican, after the Dominicans were considered the ones most responsible for the Inquisition and for encouraging integralism?): do they really represent the Catholic

Church of today, or are they not a vanguard that has lost touch with the body of the community? Does the *Catechism of the Catholic Church* say the same thing? Yes, it does. This is how it is stated in the *Catechismo degli Adulti* (Catechism for Adults), published by the Conference of Italian Bishops in 1995: "The presence of the Church in society degenerates into a confusion between the religious and civil spheres, thus compromising the purity of religion and the autonomy of the temporal reality.... The right to freedom of conscience is not sufficiently recognized, and hence the intolerance toward the Jews, the Inquisition against heretics, the forced conversions of entire peoples, the religious wars" (p. 238).

FOURTEEN

Islam

For Pope John Paul the question of Islam has proved to be the most difficult barrier. In spite of the lack of any response, he continues to come up against this barrier with three principal messages:

— Christian and Muslims are brothers under God;

— they should strive to rise above the past wars that have separated them;

— they can do this only by mutual forgiveness.

These three messages were implicitly contained in the invitation to dialogue issued by the Second Vatican Council, but it is a particular merit of Pope Wojtyla that he has spelled them out and has tried to deliver them to those to whom they are addressed.

The word "brothers," which was never used previously by a pope in addressing the followers of Islam, sounds like the promise of a change of attitude and has in fact been used in the invitation to the Muslims to participate in the days of prayer at Assisi in 1986 and 1993. To call them brothers and to invite them to a day of prayer is very likely a very personal gesture, coming from the practical genius of Pope John Paul II. He must have thought that if we can actually learn to pray together, then Christians and Muslims will cease to wage war against one another.

The call to rise above the past by purging our historical memory of the concept of two distinct "People of God" remains for the time being a global aspiration without any significant practical results. Nevertheless, the affirmation of the principle has already produced two particular historical revisions: one in regard to the Crusades and the other coming from the Conference of Spanish Bishops marking the fifth centenary of the expulsion of the Moors from Spain.

Finally, there is the call to mutual forgiveness, but up until now we have no concrete action. Nevertheless, we can cite an incident that had a great impact. A Christian martyr in our days forgave his Muslim murderer, saying that it was not his faith that prompted him to kill. Hence, when the Pope challenges Islam to forgive, he is not the mouthpiece of a weak faith striving to escape from history and the conflicts of the past, but the preacher of a Christian faith which at its very origin paid with its blood for the message of universal brotherhood. This is what lay behind the obstinacy with which Pope John Paul II opposed the Gulf War in 1990-91. But what does the world know of such a passion?

Muslim Brothers

Pope Wojtyla is the first one to call the Muslims "brothers," using the title that the Christian tradition reserves for "brothers in the faith," namely, other baptized persons. The boldness of the Pope's gesture consists in the fact that when he arrived at Kaduna, Nigeria, in 1982, he had to read his important speech to the authorities who had come to welcome him at the airport, rather than addressing the Muslim religious leaders. The scheduled meeting with the Muslims did not take place, due to dissension among them. Some of the newspaper articles even accused the Pope of being responsible, together with his predecessors, for the Crusades. But because the government authorities at the airport were also Muslims, the Pope addressed them as follows:

> All of us, Christians and Muslims, live under the sun of the one merciful God. We both believe in the one God who is the Creator of man. We acclaim God's sovereignty and we defend man's dignity as God's servant. We adore God and profess total submission to him. Thus, in a true sense, we can call one another brothers and sisters in faith in the one God (Address to the Governor and civil authorities, Kaduna, Nigeria, February 14, 1982).

Seven years later, Pope John Paul will use the expression "Muslim brothers" twice in his Apostolic Letter on the situation in Lebanon. It was issued on September 26, 1989, and in his appeal to the Muslims he used the phrase "we believers":

> As children of the God of mercy, who is our Creator and Guide but also our Judge, how can we believers allow ourselves to remain indifferent to a whole people which is dying before our very eyes? (Appeal to all Muslims on behalf of the people of Lebanon, September 26, 1989).

The most important text is the one in which Pope Wojtyla refers to the Muslims as brothers in faith, in a prayer inserted in the prayers for peace in Europe, held at Assisi in January, 1993. Both the Jews and the Muslims are saluted as sons of Abraham, and in that respect they are both our brothers in faith:

> For all those who acknowledge Abraham as their father
> in faith: Jews, Christians, Muslims: that every lack of
> understanding and every obstacle may be removed and
> they may all collaborate to work for peace *(Vigil for
> peace,* Assisi, January 10, 1993).

This prayer is unique in the Catholic liturgy. In it
the Muslims are listed last because historically they are
younger brothers in relation to Christians, born of the
lineage of Abraham, while the Jews are older brothers.
But in a certain way on that particular day (when the
eyes of the world were fixed on Bosnia and on the fate
of the Muslim population, persecuted by both Serbs and
Croats) the Muslims were first in the thoughts of the
Pope. In fact, the prayer was read in Arabic, because in
that vigil for peace the Pope wanted Europe to speak in
all its different languages, and in Europe there were already fifteen million Muslims, half of them Arabic-
speaking people.

Finish With the Wars of the Past

The most important call to Islam was made by Pope
John Paul three years later at Casablanca, where he was
able to speak to a crowd of young Muslims, the first
pope in history to do so. He invited them to move beyond the past and meet with other believers, seeking
forgiveness:

> Christians and Muslims, in general we have badly un-
> derstood each other, and sometimes, in the past, we
> have opposed and even exhausted each other in po-
> lemics and in wars.
>   I believe that, today, God invites us to change our
> old practices. We must respect each other, and also we
> must stimulate each other in good works on the path of
> God....

Dear young people, I wish that you may be able to help in thus building a world where God may have first place in order to aid and to save mankind. On this path you are assured of the esteem and the collaboration of your Catholic brothers and sisters whom I represent among you this evening.... Then, I am convinced, a world can be born where men and women of living and effective faith will sing to the glory of God and will seek to build a human society in accordance with God's will (Meeting with young Muslims, Casablanca, Morocco, August 19, 1985).

With a final invocation, "The good God is infinitely merciful" (a statement found in both the Bible and the Koran), the Pope asks, for the Muslims and the Christians, "sentiments of mercy and understanding, of pardon and reconciliation, of service and collaboration."

We Should Forgive Each Other

The message of Cardinal Arinze for the close of Ramadan in 1996 speaks of "mutual forgiveness." It was sent to the Muslims in the name of the Pope and was published in more than ten different languages, under the title, "Christians and Muslims: Beyond Tolerance":

Our relations as believers, Christians and Muslims, should go beyond mere tolerance understood simply as putting up with one another. A brother is not just to be tolerated; he is to be loved. For us as Christians and Muslims to reach beyond tolerance to reconciliation and love there is still a long way to go. As we prepare the future we cannot afford to forget the past or neglect the present....

The time has come to free our memories of the negative consequences of the past, however painful they may be, and look resolutely toward the future. The one who has given offense must repent and ask for par-

don. We need mutual pardon. Without true reconciliation we cannot commit ourselves together on behalf
of our fellow believers and for the good of the whole
world. Muslims and Christians can become, in today's
world, examples of reconciliation and instruments of
peace.

It is not only the weight of the past that has to be
taken into account. The grievous conflict in Bosnia-
Hercegovina has been falsely interpreted by some as an
example of Christian-Muslim confrontation. The war
in Southern Sudan, protracted for so many years, has
doubtless many causes, but the state of relations between Muslims and Christians can be considered as
one of many elements contributing to the conflict. In
some countries the conditions in which various religious minorities find themselves can be a source of tension. These sorry situations call for reflection on our
part, reflection carried out in God's sight, in order to
set them right.

Relations between Christians and Muslims are continually on the increase. How do we see our future? As
one of confrontation or as mere coexistence? Or
marked by mutual understanding and respect and
fruitful collaboration? Is this not what God wants of us?
But this supposes, as I have said already, mutual forgiveness from the bottom of the heart, true reconciliation and a common commitment to building a better
world for future generations. (Message of Cardinal
Francis Arinze to Muslims to mark the end of Ramadan, February 15, 1996).

"We cannot forget the past; we must both own it and
go beyond it." This is what the Cardinal said in his message. And here is an example: Archbishop Cascante of
Tarragon, Spain, president of the commission of Spanish bishops on religious affairs, stated in a solemn declaration on March 26, 1992: "There is no doubt that what
the Christians did to the Muslims and Jews in Spain in

1492 is completely contrary to that which they should
have done in accordance with the principles of our
Christian faith."

Where Forgiveness Can Lead

The "courage to forgive" is an expression from Pope
John Paul II and he used it also in reference to Islamic
extremism. But is this not the senseless talk of those
who seek consolation in words when they have been
hurt by deeds? No; it is much more than that. When the
Pope uses the word "forgiveness" in reference to Islam it
is not just an empty word. The horrible event in the
spring of 1996 has shown that this is a golden word pur-
chased with life. On May 24, 1996, a group of armed
Muslims in Algeria announced that they had "cut the
throats" of the seven Trappist monks they had seized
during the night between the 26th and 27th of March.
Then, on Pentecost Sunday, May 26, the Pope referred
to the tragedy in his Sunday message:

> Despite our deep sorrow, we thank God for the witness
> of love given by those religious. Their fidelity and con-
> stancy honor the Church and they will certainly be a
> seed of reconciliation and peace for the Algerian
> people, with whom they were in solidarity. May our
> prayers also reach their families, the Cistercian Order
> and the small ecclesial community in Algeria: in this
> tragic trial may they never lack the courage of forgive-
> ness and the strength of hope. With words from the
> Book of Genesis: "From man in regard to his fellow
> man I will demand an accounting for human life" (Gn
> 9:5), I address an appeal to all men of good will, and
> even more to those who call themselves children of
> Abraham, so that similar actions are never repeated in
> Algeria or elsewhere (Sunday message, St. Peter's, May
> 26, 1996).

To speak of forgiveness in the face of such an extreme Islamic fundamentalism would sound foolish or downright provocative if the Gospel teaching on forgiveness were not so amply demonstrated in modern times by Christians who live in Muslim lands. One extraordinary document on the spirituality of forgiveness has come to light precisely at the time of the massacre of the monks in Algeria. Their superior, foreseeing their final destiny, had sent this message to friends and relatives in France. It is dated January 1, 1994:

> If they seize me some day (and it could happen today) to become a victim of the terrorism which seems to threaten all the foreigners who live in Algeria today, I would want my community, my Church and my family to remember that I have given my life to God and to this country....
>
> I have lived long enough to consider myself an accomplice in the evil which, alas!, seems to prevail in the world and also in that which can unexpectedly happen to me. If that moment comes, I would like to have the spark of lucidity that would enable me to ask pardon of God and of my brothers in humanity, and at the same time with all my heart to pardon him who has struck me.
>
> I cannot hope for such a death. It seems important to me to declare it. In fact, I don't see how I could rejoice in the fact that a people that I love should indiscriminately be accused of my murder. It would be too high a price to pay for what is called "the grace of martyrdom".... I know well the contempt in which the Algerians are held throughout the world. I also understand the caricature of Islam which is fostered by a certain form of Islamism.
>
> It is all too easy to put one's conscience at rest by identifying this religion with the fundamentalism of its extremists. For me, Algeria and Islam are something else; they are a body and a soul....

And you, too, friend of my last moment, who will not have realized what you have done. Yes, to you also I want to say thanks and farewell.... And if it is granted to us good thieves to meet again in Paradise, it will be the will of God, our common Father. Amen!

The real question, as regards Islam, is reciprocity. I have looked but could not find any "revisions of history" on the part of any of the organisms or personalities of the Islamic world. But there are intellectuals who recognize the problem. For example, Khaled Fouad Allam has had ample opportunity to reflect on the initiatives for dialogue made by Pope John Paul II, and this is what he said: "In 1986 I took part in the interreligious day of prayer at Assisi as a member of the Islamic delegation and I heard a phrase from Wojtyla that struck me: 'We Catholics have not always been bearers of peace'.... In Islam we have not yet reached this level; there are other problems, the first of which is the economic crisis and the Islamic extremism of Indonesia and Algeria."[49]

FIFTEEN

Luther

The failure of the Catholic Church to respond to Luther's appeal for the reform of the Church is considered a fault by Pope John Paul II. This is a courageous stand, which the travelling Pope has reached by stages after fifteen years of reflection. His most important statement was made at Paderborn, Germany, on June 22, 1996, where he joined the Lutherans in an ecumenical meeting. The first step had been taken under similar circumstances at Mainz on November 17, 1980, where he spoke favorably of Martin Luther, admitting that there were faults on both sides at the time of the Protestant Reformation. Further progress was made on yet another occasion when the Pope visited a Lutheran church in Rome on December 13, 1983, and when he visited various Lutheran communities in central Europe in June of 1989. Perhaps the Lutheran question is the most significant of all the self-examinations mandated by the Pope after his encounters with persons who presented very pointed challenges.

To Do Him Justice

We shall begin with the Pope's most mature pronouncement, which was delivered at Paderborn in June, 1996:

> Today, 450 years after his death, the time that has passed permits us better to understand the person and the work of the German reformer and to do justice to him. It has not only been the research of important Evangelical and Catholic scholars that has helped to sketch a more complete and complex picture of Martin Luther's personality. The Lutheran-Catholic dialogue has also made an important contribution to overcoming old polemics and to coming closer to a common viewpoint.
>
> Luther's thought was characterized by a strong emphasis on the individual, which weakened the awareness of the community's requirements. Luther's call for Church reform in its original meaning was an appeal for repentance and renewal, which must begin in the life of every individual. Nevertheless, there are many reasons why division arose from this beginning. Among these is that failure in the Catholic Church for which Pope Adrian VI had already grieved in moving words; the interference of political and economic interests; and also Luther's own passion, which led him well beyond his initial intention to a radical criticism of the Catholic Church, her structure and her doctrine. We are all guilty. For this reason we are all invited to repentance and we all need to be purified again and again by the Lord (Ecumenical celebration, Paderborn, Germany, June 22, 1996).

Just prior to the ecumenical meeting, the Pope addressed the representatives of the Lutheran Church and explained to them why he admired Martin Luther, in spite of his personal limitations and the doctrinal questions that still need to be clarified:

After centuries of alienation and opposition, his memory permits us today to recognize more clearly the great importance of his request for a theology close to Sacred Scripture and a spiritual renewal of the Church (Meeting with representatives of the Evangelical Churches, Paderborn, Germany, June 22, 1996).

Such was the desired reformation to which the Catholic Church had not responded, and note that the Pope did not say that "the members of the Catholic Church" did not respond, but "the Catholic Church."

Deep Religiosity

In a letter to Cardinal Willebrands, President of the Secretariat for Christian Unity, on the occasion of the fifth centenary of the birth of Martin Luther (1983), Pope Wojtyla acknowledged the "deep religious feeling" of the reformer and the degree of responsibility on the part of "the authorities of the Catholic Church" for the "rupture of Church unity":

> The scientific researches of Evangelical and Catholic scholars...have led to the delineation of a more complete and more differentiated picture of Luther's personality.... Consequently, there is clearly outlined the deep religious feeling of Luther, who was driven with burning passion by the question of eternal salvation. Likewise, it has become clear that the breach of Church unity cannot be traced back either to a lack of understanding on the part of the authorities of the Catholic Church, or solely to Luther's lack of understanding of true Catholicism, even if both factors played their role.
>
> The decisions taken had much deeper roots. In the dispute about the relationship between faith and tradition, there were at stake fundamental questions on the correct interpretation and the reception of the Christian faith which had within them a potential for ecclesial

division which cannot be explained by purely historical reasons.

Therefore a twofold effort is necessary, both in regard to Martin Luther and also for the re-establishment of unity. In the first place it is necessary to continue an accurate historical work. By means of an investigation without preconceived ideas, motivated solely by a search for the truth, one must arrive at a true image of the reformer, of the whole period of the Reformation, and of the persons involved in it. Fault, where it exists, must be recognized, wherever it may lie. Where controversy has clouded one's view, that view must be corrected independently of either party. Besides, we must not allow ourselves to be guided by the intention of setting ourselves up as judges of history, but solely by the motive of understanding better what happened and of becoming messengers of truth. Only by placing ourselves unreservedly in an attitude of purification by means of the truth can we find a shared interpretation of the past and at the same time reach a new point of departure for the dialogue of today.

And this is precisely the second thing which is necessary. The clarification of history which looks back on the past for its significance that still lasts, must go *pari passu* with the dialogue of faith in which at present we are engaged in the quest for unity. This dialogue—according to the Evangelical-Lutheran confessional writings—has its solid basis in that which unites us even after the separation, namely, in the Word of Scripture, in the Confessions of faith, and in the Councils of the ancient Church. I therefore trust, Eminence, that on these bases and in this spirit the Secretariat for Unity, under your guidance, will carry on this dialogue begun in Germany with great seriousness already before the Second Vatican Council, and that it will do so in fidelity to the faith freely given, which implies penitence and a readiness to learn from listening (Letter to Cardinal Willebrands for the fifth centenary of the birth of Martin Luther, November 5, 1983).

The foregoing text is crucial for understanding the criteria desired by Pope John Paul for the "clarification of history" with a view to a "shared interpretation of the past," for fostering an "attitude of purification," so that "where controversy has beclouded one's view, that view may be corrected." One could say that this contains in a nutshell the entire pedagogy of the self-examination at the end of the millennium which will be developed in the years that follow. This attests to the ecumenical format of that pedagogy.

Excommunication Ends With Death

The need to admit faults had already been emphasized at the meeting in Mainz in November of 1980. The Pope acknowledged the blame that was due to the Catholic side in the tensions that led to the "unfortunate divisions among Christians":

> I recall at this moment that, in 1510-1511, Martin Luther came to Rome as a pilgrim to the tombs of the Princes of the Apostles, but also as one seeking and questioning. Today I come to you, to the spiritual heirs of Martin Luther. I come as a pilgrim. With this pilgrimage I come to set, in a changed world, a sign of union in the central mystery of our faith....
>
> Allow me to express right at the beginning of our talk what particularly moves me. I do so in connection with the testimony of the Letter to the Romans, that writing which was absolutely decisive for Martin Luther. "This Letter is the real masterpiece of the New Testament and the purest Gospel," he wrote in 1522.
>
> In the school of the Apostle to the Gentiles we can become aware that we all need conversion.... "Let us no more pass judgment on one another" (Rm 14:13). Let us rather recognize our guilt (Meeting with representatives of the Council of the German Evangelical Churches, Mainz, Germany, November 17, 1980).

Note that here the pilgrim Pope Wojtyla resembles the pilgrim Martin Luther and he even quotes a Lutheran text from 1522, a text which Martin Luther published after he was excommunicated (the papal bull *Exsurge Domine* of Leo X, which announced the excommunication, was actually dated 1520). As a matter of fact, Pope John Paul no longer considered him as excommunicated, because nine years later, during a visit to the Scandinavian countries, he stated that "excommunication ends with the death of the individual" (Copenhagen, June 6, 1989).[50]

Also on the occasion of the Pope's visit to the Lutheran Church in Rome on December 11, 1983, he made a significant gesture of recognition by reading the beautiful prayer for Church unity, composed by Martin Luther at the end of his life:

> We pray to you, O Lord, and we beseech you, we poor sinners, that through your Holy Spirit you will to restore unity to that which is shattered, reunite that which is divided and make it one. Grant that we may return to your one eternal truth, leaving behind all divisions, so that the one thought and one sentiment will lead us to you, Lord Jesus Christ.[51]

To summarize: Pope Wojtyla did not ask pardon of Luther and he did not refer to the excommunication, the effects of which he considered finished. The Holy Father is looking for a "new and general evaluation of the many questions that come from Luther and his message." The most important thing is to recognize that the basic cause of the division was the lack of a Catholic response to the call of Luther for the reform of the Church. With this admission, Wojtyla, the first non-Italian pope in modern times, boldly aligns himself with Adrian VI, the last non-Italian pope of the Renaissance, who in 1522 tried to engage the Church of Rome in a program of reform in answer to the Lutheran movement. We have already seen that Pope John Paul II actually quoted Pope Adrian VI at Paderborn.

Could Pope Wojtyla say more about Luther today? Perhaps he could say in his own name what Pope Paul VI had Cardinal Willebrands say when he addressed the fifth assembly of the Lutheran Federation in July, 1970: "Luther is our common teacher on the doctrine of justification."[52]

As a matter of fact, Pope John Paul has personally recognized Martin Luther as a "common master." As we have seen, he used a prayer by Luther at an ecumenical celebration. He said that Luther's religious spirit, his request for a theology close to Scripture, and his call for the reform of the Church were providential actions. They would have been decisive if the Catholic Church had been willing to respond. It is certainly possible that Pope Wojtyla would say in his own name what Pope Montini had Cardinal Willebrands say at that meeting with the Lutheran Federation, but unlike his predecessor, Pope John Paul could not afford to be suspected of yielding too much to Protestantism.

SIXTEEN

The Mafia

P ope John Paul II has spoken twice about the Mafia, or rather of the members of the Mafia, in regard to the responsibility of the Church: once in Calabria (1983) and another time in Rome, when he addressed the bishops of Sicily (1995). On other occasions, when he visited Sicily in 1993 and 1994, he cried out against the Mafia, branding it as the work of the devil and threatening it with the judgment of God. These outbursts marked a change in the image of the Church in relation to that phenomenon, a change that was understood by everyone, including the members of the Mafia. Here we shall limit ourselves to a consideration of the two interventions in which the Pope invited the Church to an examination of conscience and to repentance.

The Church Cannot Remain Silent

When Pope John Paul spoke of the Mafia at Cosenza in Calabria in 1983, he did so with words from the Bible. He took his cue from a passage in Isaiah in which the Chosen People are compared to a rebellious vineyard that brought forth wild grapes (Is 5:1-2):

> We, who are the vineyard of the Lord, how many wild grapes we have produced instead of good grapes! How many feuds and vendettas, shedding of blood, thefts, robberies, kidnappings, injustices and violence of every kind!... The Church cannot remain silent in the face of these problems; she cannot be withdrawn or indifferent. The Church and all Christians have a duty to put themselves in the front lines of those who denounce injustices, and especially to cultivate a strong moral, social and political conscience that will produce concrete initiatives.... The Church in Calabria should be present to the social reality of this earth. She should help the men and women of Calabria to reinvigorate the sense of one's rights and duties, the moral sense of the rights of others, the sense of justice and solidarity in human and social relationships.... Our beloved Calabria is the vineyard of the Lord! May it always be loved this way by God as was the vineyard of which Isaiah speaks! (Cosenza, October 6, 1983).

Pope John Paul does not use the word "Mafia" or the word "*'ndrangheta,*" which is used in Calabria to designate the Mafia, but his enumeration of the evils produced in the "vineyard of the Lord," meaning Calabria, is a detailed inventory of the activities of the "*'ndrangheta*": "feuds and vendettas, shedding of blood, thefts, robberies, kidnapping."

A Courageous Examination of Conscience

Another text that is even more explicit in its reference to the Mafia and in its call for a change from the past is contained in the discourse of June 22, 1995, when the Pope addressed a group of pilgrims from Sicily. Here he invites them to an examination of conscience in view of the third millennium:

> A cry goes out from my heart to Agrigento at the end of the eucharistic celebration...prompted by the thought that Sicily, so rich in humanity and talent, in resources and in faith, for too long...has been pointed at and denigrated as if its criminal organizations were its outstanding feature. That cry comes forth from a confidence in the human and Christian qualities of a people illustrious for the rich patrimony of their past history and deserving of respect for their many sufferings at the present time, sufferings which have not been able to make them lose the will to redeem their good name.
>
> Dear Sicilians, the moment has come to make an appeal to every good resolution. On approaching the new millennium I have frequently invited the entire Church to make a courageous examination of conscience, so that the power and grace of God will be able to open a new page in history. I propose the same to you, dear faithful of Sicily. You should make a vigorous pledge to persevere in the effort to give your land a new face, worthy of the culture and Christian civilization that has always marked your island. This is what I have wanted to cry out to Agrigento.
>
> The Mafia was born of a society that is spiritually incapable of recognizing the wealth of which the people of Sicily are bearers. Therefore I repeat to you today what I said during the course of my last visit to Catania: "Be happy, Sicily. Be aware of your wealth, and especially of that truly inestimable wealth of your faith in Christ." You will be free if you have the courage to take your stand at the side of the unique Lord of history (Address to the pilgrimage from Sicily, St. Peter's, June 22, 1995).

That the Church is at fault for what the Mafia has done, at least because of "negative complicity" (meaning to be culpably passive), and because of the Church's equivocal attitude, was stated publicly by Cardinal Pappalardo of Palermo, a courageous fighter against the Cosa Nostra of Sicily. As vice-president of the Conference of Italian Bishops, he addressed them at Loreto on April 10, 1985:

> As a bishop among the bishops of Italy, I think I can speak in the name of all in asking mercy of the Lord, who is good and loves mankind, in confessing whatever may be our faults in confronting the world. And I think that I can ask for forgiveness in the name of all our local churches for all that we could have done or could have done better and did not do so.... Whether it is a question of small offenses or organized crime or political scandals or something else, such as terrorism and the Mafia, it is always something that involves the Church, over and above the funerals to which she has become accustomed in recent times! It is a question of confessing the sin of complicity, at least in the negative sense, or of a certain degree of equivocation in what the ecclesial communities have committed or omitted.[53]

This statement by Cardinal Pappalardo is unique in the history of the Conference of Italian Bishops. It brings the Conference to the point of asking for forgiveness, even before Pope John Paul had made it a password. However, the Italian Bishops did not dare to do so even after the Pope had suggested it. Nor did the Conference do so during the Third National Convention of the Church in Italy ten years later (November, 1995), although it was described as "an excellent occasion for publicly asking pardon for all the compromises and delays which cannot be justified in the light of the Gospel and of charity."[54]

Even earlier, at the end of 1982, Archbishop Vincenzo Fagiolo, now a cardinal and at the time president of

Caritas and vice-president of the Conference of Bishops, had stated that the crimes of the Mafia and the Camorra cry out to heaven for vengeance: "The crimes of the Mafia and the Camorra are excessive. They cry out to God for vengeance and they weigh on our conscience. The entire Church in Italy ought to feel responsible for so many murders and each of the ecclesial communities ought to be ashamed to have in its midst a Christian who is not even worthy to be called a man. Therefore it should morally reject him, exclude him and not let him be helped by anyone...as long as he has not amended his life."[55]

SEVENTEEN

Racism

P ope Wojtyla has frequently spoken of racism and condemned its various forms, such as anti-Semitism, apartheid, the caste system in India, discrimination against the Indians in South America, tribal struggles, oppression of the aborigines, treatment of Blacks. In each case he has acknowledged the responsibility of Catholics or at least implied it. We have provided some detailed documentation in the chapters on the Jews and on Indians, and we shall give further details in the chapters on Rwanda and the treatment of Blacks. What is lacking is a specific pronouncement on the responsibility of the Church in regard to the complex phenomenon of racism, but there is a Vatican document, published with his approval in 1989 which is a self-accusation of racist behavior in the course of history and in the world today:

> Historically, racial prejudice, in the strict sense of the word, that is, awareness of the biologically determined superiority of one's own race or ethnic group with respect to others, developed above all from the practices of colonization and slavery at the dawn of the modern era. In rapidly considering the history of earlier major

civilizations in the West, as in the East, in the North as in the South, one can already find unjust and discriminatory behavior, but one cannot in every case speak about racism as such....

The Christian Middle Ages also made distinctions among peoples on the basis of religious criteria: Christians, Jews and "infidels." It is for this reason that, within "Christendom," the Jews, considered the tenacious witnesses of a refusal to believe in Christ, were often the object of serious humiliations, accusations and proscriptions....

If the great navigators of the fifteenth and sixteenth centuries were free from racial prejudices, the soldiers and traders did not have the same respect for others: they killed in order to take possession of the land: reduced first the "Indians" and then the Blacks to slavery in order to exploit their work. At the same time they began to develop a racist theory in order to justify their actions.

The popes did not delay in reacting. On June 2, 1537, the Bull *Sublimis Deus* of Paul III denounced those who held that "the inhabitants of the West Indies and the southern continents should be treated like irrational animals and used exclusively for our profit and our service..." The directives of the Holy See were extremely clear even if, unhappily, their application soon met with difficulties. Later Urban VIII went so far as to excommunicate those who kept Indians as slaves.

For their part, theologians and missionaries had already come to the defense of the indigenous people. The resolute commitment on the side of the Indians of Bartolomé de Las Casas, a soldier who became a priest, then a Dominican religious and bishop, was soon taken up by many other missionaries.... The work of Las Casas is one of the first contributions to the doctrine of universal human rights, based on the dignity of the person, regardless of his or her ethnic or religious affiliation. In the same way, Francisco de Vitoria and

Francisco Suárez, pioneers of the rights of peoples, developed this same doctrine of the basic equality of all persons and of all peoples.... However, the close dependency of the clergy of the New World on the patronage system meant that the Church was not always able to implement the necessary pastoral decisions....

Because of its constant concern for the deeper respect for indigenous peoples, the Apostolic See again and again insisted that a careful distinction be made between the work of evangelization and colonial imperialism, with which the former risked being confused.... In places where missionaries were more closely dependent on political powers, it was more difficult for them to curb the colonists' attempt to dominate. At times they even gave it encouragement on the basis of false interpretations of the Bible....

The Church has the sublime vocation of realizing, first of all within herself, the unity of humankind over and above any ethnic, cultural, national, social or other divisions in order to signify precisely that such divisions are now obsolete, having been abolished by the cross of Christ.... The repeated failures due to people's insensitivity and the sins of her own members can in no way weaken what the Church has the vocation and mission to accomplish by divine mandate....

If people, and human communities, are all equal in dignity, that does not mean that they all have, at a given moment, equal physical abilities, cultural endowments, intellectual and moral strengths or that they are at the same stage of development. Equality does not mean uniformity. It is important to recognize the diversity and complementarity of one another's cultural riches and moral qualities.... No human group, however, can boast of having a natural superiority over others or of exercising any discrimination that affects the basic rights of the person....

In her denunciations of racism, however, the Church tries to maintain an evangelical attitude with

regard to all. This is undoubtedly her particular gift....
The Church wants first and foremost to change racist
attitudes, including those within her own communities.... Despite the sinful limitations of her members,
yesterday and today, she is aware of having been constituted a witness to Christ's charity on earth, a sign and
instrument of the unity of humankind (Pontifical Commission *"Justitia et Pax,"* November 3, 1988).

We have said that this is the only chapter in which we
have not incorporated any text pronounced by the Pope
in which he made an explicit confession of fault. However, we did find a beautiful statement that amounts to
an indirect reference to the topic we are discussing.

In September of 1987, during a visit to the United
States, the Pope was in New Orleans, and he met with
representatives of Black American Catholics. At that
time the only Black bishop at the head of a diocese was
Joseph Lawson Howze of Biloxi, Louisiana (though
there were ten other Black bishops in the country as
auxiliaries). In presenting the group to the Holy Father,
Bishop Howze stated that "in the Church also there is a
racism that prevents the full development of Catholic
leadership among the Blacks." He also stated that it is
difficult for a Black person to adhere to the Catholic
Church because he perceives it as "a white Church that
is also European American." Hence, the Black person
fears that if he joins it, he will have to "abandon his own
racial heredity and his own people."[56]

The Pope's response greatly impressed the assembly
and came across as a substantial admission of responsibility for the past and for the present as regards the
practice of racism:

It is important to realize that there is no Black Church,
no White Church, no American Church; but there is

and must be in the one Church of Jesus Christ, a home for Blacks, Whites, Americans, every culture and race (Meeting with Afro-Americans, New Orleans, September 15, 1987).

In the relationship between races and cultures, Pope Wojtyla proposes the following actions: admission of faults, pardon, and reconciliation. It is the same pedagogy that he has applied to the field of ecumenism. During the meeting in New Orleans, he addressed Black Catholics as follows: "Continue to inspire us by your desire to forgive—as Jesus forgave—and by your desire to be reconciled with all the people of this nation, even those who would unjustly deny you the full exercise of your human rights." Later on, he advocated the application of the same criterion during a visit to Zambia in May, 1989, in one of his numerous protests against the apartheid of South Africa:

> As one of the leading nations in Africa, at the cost of great labor you have succeeded in building a society of amicable relations among people of every race. This must be your response to the unacceptable system of apartheid. Racism has been condemned, but it does not suffice merely to condemn it. It is also necessary to banish the conditions that are dictated by fear. It is necessary to achieve reconciliation (Address at the airport, Kuanda, Zambia, May 2, 1989).

Even more forceful, or at least more direct, is the admission of the sin of racism in the area of ecumenism. The final document issued by the Worldwide Ecumenical Assembly held at Seoul, Korea, in March of 1990, contains the following statement: "Let us make an alliance to confess and repent of our complicity, voluntary or not, in the racism that permeates the Church and society."

EIGHTEEN

Rwanda

Rwanda is a good example of the fact that Pope John Paul recognizes not only the injustices of the past, but those of the present as well. Among his interventions concerning the tribal wars in this country, we shall report the two most dramatic ones: the Sunday allocution in 1994, in which he admits the responsibility of Catholics for genocide, and the letter of 1996 in which he invites those Catholics responsible for the massacre to submit to the legal process.

All Will Have to Give an Account

A pope who declares the responsibility of Catholics for a massacre that is actually going on is an historical novelty. Here are his words:

> It is a question of a true and authentic genocide, for which, unfortunately, Catholics are also responsible. I am close to these people in their suffering and I would like to address again the conscience of all those who planned this massacre and carried it out. They are carrying this country toward the abyss! All of them must

answer to history and to God for their crimes. Enough blood! God expects of all the people of Rwanda, together with their neighboring countries, a moral reawakening: the courage of pardon and brotherhood (Sunday message transmitted from Gemelli Hospital in Rome, May 15, 1994).

At other times individual Christians have denounced the sin of an entire Catholic community. For example, Bernanos spoke in the name of all against the role of the Church in the Spanish civil war. The fact that it is now the Pope who speaks out is a sign of the times. Perhaps this will be the salvation of Catholicism in Africa, which has grown so rapidly but is now less African and perhaps less Christian.

Moreover, the words of Pope John Paul show his personal intervention in the drama of Rwanda. He sent this message from his hospital bed at a time when he should have been presenting to the Church his program for the Great Jubilee at the end of the millennium. His fall on April 29 had made it necessary for him to start out on the road to recovery for the sixth time. His stay in Gemelli Hospital caused him to postpone, among other activities, the extraordinary Consistory which had been scheduled from May to June. It was in view of that Consistory that he had sent the memorandum to the cardinals, of which we have already spoken, and it was in that memorandum that he launched the proposal of an examination of conscience at the end of the present millennium concerning the historical faults of the Church. And behold, there erupts in the Church yet another form of violence that adds fresh blood to the terrible catalog of crimes. The Pope responds immediately to this new crisis. He is, in fact, the first one to respond to his own proposal for an examination of conscience.

To Catholics Who Have Sinned

In the space of two years the genocide had resulted in the death of more than a million persons in a general population of eight million, of whom 45% were Catholics. Among those massacred there were three bishops and hundreds of priests, religious and catechists. One out of four priests was murdered. And often the great slaughters that took place in the churches turned them into "slaughter-houses of the innocent," as Cardinal Etchegaray stated on June 26, 1994. He had been sent to Rwanda to represent the Holy Father, who was recuperating in Gemelli Hospital. Sometimes the priests and religious were murdered because they spoke out against the genocide, but sometimes they were among those responsible for the massacres. There were also ecclesiastical prelates who were being sought by the International Tribunal for crimes in Rwanda. The Pope referred to guilty Catholics in his letter to the president of the Conference of Bishops in Rwanda, marking the second anniversary of the beginning of the genocide in April of 1994:

> I once again reverence the memory of all the victims of this tragedy, especially the bishops, the pastors and the other faithful of the Church, and I ask the Lord to show them mercy.
>
> At a time when your country is seeking ways of reconciliation and peace, I fervently encourage all its children to discover new hope in Christ. The infinite mercy of God, who forgives everyone in every circumstance, is fully manifested in him....
>
> The State must face a great and demanding challenge: it has the essential duty to give justice to all. And I would like to say again that justice and truth must go hand in hand when it is a question of bringing to light

the responsibilities for the tragedy experienced by your country. The Church as such cannot be held responsible for the faults of her members who acted against the law of the Gospel; they will be called to account for their acts. All the members of the Church who sinned during the genocide must have the courage to bear the consequences of the deeds they committed against God and against their neighbor.

I am thinking most especially of the many prisoners waiting to be sentenced, of those who have lost all of their loved ones or their possessions and are waiting for justice to be done to them, of refugees within the nation and those, so numerous, who are waiting beyond the borders to be able to return to their country in safety and dignity....

I invite you all, bishops, priests, religious, lay people, of different ethnic origins, to turn to God with a sincere heart, to forgive and be reconciled (Letter to Bishop Thaddeus Ntihinyurwa, president of the Conference of Bishops of Rwanda, March 14, 1996).

Pope Wojtyla had spoken of genocide on other occasions, admitting that there were also Catholics who were responsible, but this time he said more. He told the Catholics who had sinned that they should "bear the consequences for the deeds they committed." He also urges the State to render justice to all.

These were compelling statements; first of all because of the courage with which the Pope put his finger on the spot (among the accused there were priests who fled the country) and secondly, because he challenged the politics of the regime. To invite the State to render justice is equivalent to calling for the legal proceedings which the Patriotic Front—the Tutsi military government in power since July, 1994—had deferred *sine die*, while some fifty thousand prisoners were awaiting trial.

The Tutsi military government had made part of its propaganda the accusation that the Church had supported the previous regime, which was controlled by the Hutu tribe, and had even aided that regime in the genocide. It is in view of this situation that the distinction made by the Pope is important. The Church as such is not responsible for what individual members do; they should undergo civil trial.

But do the denunciations by the Pope and his invitation to reconciliation make any sense? His voice is certainly a force in a Catholic community involved in a similar tragedy, but what can a Polish Pope know about Rwanda? Cardinal Etchegaray had said in a message to the people of Rwanda, dated July 2, 1994: "I do not understand, and no one in the world can understand, nor can any of you understand what has happened to you."

Fortunately voices are not lacking in Rwanda that are in agreement with the Pope. The strongest voice has been that of Bishop Gahamanyi of Butare in a pastoral letter addressed to his people, published a year after the beginning of the genocide:

> We have become a reason for shame to God and to the name of his Son Jesus Christ.... Some Christians have killed and also tortured others. They have persecuted their own neighbors, our Christian brothers like ourselves, without any fault on their part, but only because they are as God created them.... Some Christians have lacked any respect for the human person: they have stripped individuals naked before sadistically killing them; they have inflicted great suffering on them; they have violated young persons and mothers; they have left their victims without burial; they have taken off their clothing; they have turned the dogs loose to chase after the refugees.... No tribe has been spared involvement in the horrors of genocide; one could say

that they have vied with one another in zeal (Pastoral letter of Bishop Jean Baptiste Gahamanyi of Butare, in *L'Osservatore Romano*, May 11, 1995).

This is not a case of wisdom after the event. Notice how the Bishop of Kabgayi, the prelate most responsible for the Catholic community in Rwanda and the president of the Conference of Bishops, on both counts the mediator for reconciliation, reacted in an interview at the beginning of the killing, just a few days before he himself was murdered:

> After ninety-four years of evangelization, these massacres are proof of our failure. Various priests in my diocese have seen many of their parishioners brandishing the machete and destroying the very places of worship. That is the terrible truth. The people have not assimilated Christian values. It is necessary to begin again, with new methods.... We realize that our mistake has been to have practiced mass evangelization. There have been many baptisms but few changes in the manner of living.[57]

Nor did the Pope see the genocide as a flash of lightning in a clear blue sky. He had visited Burundi and Rwanda in September of 1990 and repeatedly he was made aware of the endemic drama of tribal warfare. The Rwandan refugees of Tutsi background had sent a message to Rome before the Pope's visit, denouncing the fact that all the bishops were Hutu and that, in addition to the political discrimination in their country, there was great discrimination within the Church. At the stadium in Kigali the young people had asked the Pope: "Do you know that racism is raging in Rwanda, even in the bosom of the Church?" Pope John Paul responded:

> To harbor racist sentiments is contrary to the message of Christ, because the neighbor that Jesus commands

us to love is not only the person in my social group, my religion or my nation. My neighbor is every person that I meet on my path.

A similar idea concerning the situation in Rwanda, touching the horrors of genocide and Christian witness, was expressed by Archbishop Giuseppe Bertello, the nuncio at Kigali since 1991: "Perhaps we should reconsider our methods of evangelization. There has been an explosion of conversions, perhaps excessively so. We shall study the problem." The participation of Christians in the murders, the Archbishop continues, "is a sorrow that has afflicted the Church throughout the entire course of this civil war, which began many years ago and not on April 6, 1994, as the rest of the world believes. But we should not forget that there have been many acts of heroism: Hutu who have saved Tutsi and vice versa.... We have never ceased to speak of conciliation and national unity. But in the seminaries the tension between the two groups is evident, and this is inevitable."[58]

A thorough examination of the type of evangelization used in Africa by the missionaries and the indigenous Church was suggested also by Cardinal Hyacinthe Thiandoum at the Synod on the Church in Africa (1994). He referred in particular to the Church in Burundi and in Rwanda: "These two countries are the ones that have the highest percentage of Catholics in Africa. We synodal Fathers are asking ourselves what kind of Christian faith is prevalent in these two countries. If our evangelization does not lead to conversion, if it doesn't profoundly change hearts and minds, that is, the manner of judging oneself and the world, then our every effort is in vain. It will be gone by tomorrow."[59]

NINETEEN

Eastern Schism

The heart of Pope Wojtyla beats in unison with the East. His most forceful and frequent mea culpa pertains to the division and separation of the Eastern Churches. We can report on four texts that were issued in the last five years. Two of them are part of an important document such as an Encyclical or Apostolic Letter; one of them is from a mutual declaration co-signed by Patriarch Bartholemew of Constantinople; the fourth one was pronounced during an ecumenical celebration with the Orthodox Church in Poland in 1991. This last text is perhaps the most important because it is chronologically the first and it contains the substance of what is found in the others.

The concentration of these confessions of fault in recent years is significant. They mark an awareness of the increased difficulty of achieving union with the Eastern Churches since the interruption of dialogue following the fall of the Communist regime. Consequently, we shall begin our commentary with the Polish text. During the previous thirteen years of his pontificate, Pope John Paul was motivated by the belief that the desired union with the East was close. When he visited Istanbul in

November of 1979, Patriarch Dimitrios I of Constantinople had said: "May the dawn of this new millennium rise on a Church that has achieved full unity." But because of subsequent difficulties, Pope John Paul seems to have realized that the path to unity must be a penitential way or one of mutual pardon.

We Have All Made Mistakes

These are important words, but what is also significant is the place where they were pronounced and why they were spoken. The place is Poland, in the Orthodox cathedral at Bialystok, a few miles from the border of Belarus. The Nazis had completely destroyed Bialystok during the Second World War and had exterminated the population, especially the Jews. For centuries it had been a place of wars between Christians, alternating between Orthodox and Catholic, depending on whether the ruler was the Catholic king of Poland or the Orthodox czar of Russia. The Orthodox cathedral was chosen as the place for the ecumenical meeting, during which Pope John Paul gave his address. The cathedral was constructed on the site of the former Catholic cathedral of the Eastern rite, which had been demolished by the czarist government.

Pope Wojtyla had participated in ecumenical meetings in numerous churches of other Christian denominations. For example, he visited Lutheran churches in Rome and in Salzburg, the Orthodox cathedral of Al Fanar in Istanbul, the Anglican cathedrals at Canterbury and at Toronto, the Lutheran churches at Strasbourg, Trondheim in Norway, Rejkjavik in Iceland, Turku in Finland, Roskilde in Denmark, Uppsala in Sweden, Riga in Latvia and numerous others. But until that time there had been no visit to any non-Catholic church that was so significant and meaningful as the one in which the Pope gave the following message:

Standing before the Lord during this solemn and sublime prayer in which the invocation, "Lord, have mercy on us," has frequently resounded, we cannot fail to admit in all humility that in the past the spirit of evangelical brotherhood has not always prevailed. The sad experiences of the past still live in the memory of all. We all bear the yoke of historical faults; we have all made mistakes. If we say that we are without sin, we deceive ourselves, and the truth is not in us. There is fault on all sides, regardless of the degree, and it can be overcome by the acknowledgment of one's own culpability before the Lord and by mutual forgiveness. With profound and sincere sorrow let us admit this before God today, asking him to forgive us: Lord, have mercy on us!

Mindful of the words of the Lord's Prayer, "and forgive us our sins as we forgive those who have sinned against us," let us, in a spirit of mutual reconciliation, forgive each other for the wrongs we have suffered in the past in order to form our mutual relations in a new and authentically evangelical way and to build a better future for the reconciled Churches (Meeting with the Orthodox, Bialystok, Poland, June 5, 1991).

Fervently Asking Forgiveness

Speaking to Eastern Christians at Bialystok, Pope John Paul said, "We have all made mistakes," but in spite of his appeal for reciprocal forgiveness, the Eastern Christians seem to distance themselves from the Catholic Church more and more each year, thus shattering the Pope's hope for a quick reunion of the two Christian traditions.

With the fall of Communism, the tension between the Orthodox Christians and the Catholics of the Eastern rite (Uniate Catholics) came to the surface in the Ukraine and in Romania; the Serbian-Croatian war exposed the great rift with the patriarchate of Serbia; the assignment of Catholic bishops within the Russian territory definitively blocked any dialogue with the Patriarch of Moscow. So, in spite of the fall of Communism, Pope John Paul has not been able to visit any country in which the Orthodox Church has control. At one time it was because the governments did not wish it; now it is because the "sister churches" do not wish it. This gave rise to a renewed appeal to the Orthodox Churches in the Apostolic Letter, *Orientale Lumen*, promulgated in May of 1995. So the Pope has taken the initiative, putting himself even more clearly on an equal level, looking beyond "any wrong suffered or inflicted," and urging "courageous steps and creativity":

> In the course of the 1,000 years now drawing to a close, even more than in the first millennium, ecclesial communion has been painfully wounded, "a fact for which, often enough, men of both sides were to blame." Such wounds openly contradict the will of Christ and are a cause of scandal to the world. It is necessary to make amends for them and earnestly to beseech Christ's forgiveness.
>
> The sin of our separation is very serious.... Christian brothers and sisters who together had suffered persecution are regarding one another with suspicion and fear just when prospects and hopes of greater freedom are appearing. Is this not a new, serious risk of sin which we must all make every effort to overcome, if we want the peoples who are seeking the God of love to be able to find him more easily instead of being scandalized anew by our wounds and conflicts?... We have deprived the world of a joint witness that could perhaps

have avoided so many tragedies and even changed the course of history (Apostolic Letter, *Orientale Lumen*, May 2, 1995).

We Invite All to Forgive

Here we see that the word describing reciprocal forgiveness is reformulated in the declaration co-authored by the Pope and the Patriarch of Constantinople. The document was released at the end of the Patriarch's visit in June, 1995:

> In this perspective we urge our faithful, Catholics and Orthodox, to reinforce the spirit of brotherhood which stems from the one baptism and from participation in the sacramental life. In the course of history and in the more recent past there have been attacks and acts of oppression on both sides. As we prepare, on this occasion, to ask the Lord for his great mercy, we invite all to forgive one another and to express a firm will that a new relationship of brotherhood and active collaboration will be established.
>
> Such a spirit should encourage both Catholics and Orthodox, especially where they live side by side, to a more intense collaboration in the cultural, spiritual, pastoral, educational and social fields, avoiding any temptation to undue zeal for their own community to the disadvantage of the other. May the good of Christ's Church always prevail! Mutual support and the exchange of gifts can only make pastoral activity itself more effective and our witness to the Gospel we desire to proclaim more transparent.
>
> We maintain that a more active and concerted collaboration will also facilitate the Church's influence in promoting peace and justice in situations of political or ethnic conflict. The Christian faith has unprecedented possibilities for solving humanity's tensions and enmity.
>
> In meeting one another, the Pope of Rome and the

ecumenical Patriarch have prayed for the unity of all Christians. In their prayers, they have included all the baptized who are incorporated into Christ, and they have asked for an ever deeper fidelity to his Gospel for the various communities.

They bear in their heart a concern for all humanity, without any discrimination according to race, color, language, ideology or religion.

They therefore encourage dialogue, not only between the Christian Churches but also with the various religions, and above all, with those that are monotheistic.... May the Lord heal the wounds tormenting humanity today and hear our prayers and those of our faithful for peace in our Churches and in all the world (Common declaration of John Paul II and the Patriarch Bartholomew, June 29, 1995).

The Courage to Forgive

Finally, here is the application of the path of repentance or mutual forgiveness to the Uniate Church:

May the perspective of the forthcoming Great Jubilee of the year 2000 bring about in everyone an attitude of humility, capable of effecting "the necessary purification of past memories" through prayer and conversion of heart, so as to help people to ask and give mutual forgiveness for the misunderstandings of centuries past.... At the same time let us also ardently implore the Holy Spirit that the time may be shortened for all believers in Christ to come to glorify the Trinity together with one voice (cf. Rm 15:6). An indispensable condition for such a joyful event is that the courage to forgive will mature in the hearts of everyone; this too is a grace to be implored with tireless perseverance (Apostolic Letter for the 350th anniversary of the Union of Uzhhorod, April 18, 1996).

The healing of historical memories is especially difficult when it pertains to the question of Church unity, but the Orthodox Churches did initially intend to collaborate. This was stated in the document composed by the International Commission for Theological Dialogue between the Catholic and the Orthodox Churches: "There should be offered to all an honest and global presentation of history that will move toward a concordant and even common historiography of the two Churches. It would help to dissipate the mutual prejudices and prevent the use of history in a polemical manner. Such a presentation would make both parties aware that the faults that led to division must be shared and that they have left deep wounds on both sides."[60]

TWENTY

History of the Papacy

The history of the papacy could give any pope a reason for repentance. And not only its past history, but also the papacy in modern times, when we consider, for example, the wealth of the Church, the Swiss Guard, diplomacy and relations with the State, the title of the pope as Sovereign Pontiff, and even to some extent the doctrine on papal infallibility.

In order to avoid any "unnecessary scandal," it would be well if the Pope would "turn the Vatican into a museum and move to the gates of Rome." That was the suggestion made by the Swiss theologian, Hans Urs von Balthasar, whom Pope John Paul II had named a cardinal. The same von Balthasar also maintained that priests, bishops and popes should give up their titles, which are "antiquated and meaningless in a Christian sense." For example, he maintained that the titles "father, abbot *(abba)*, pope *(papa* in Italian) are contrary to the teaching in Matthew 23:9: 'Do not call anyone on earth your father.'" Moreover, the word "infallible" applied to the Church and to the pope was always unacceptable to von Balthasar "because men are always fallible."[61]

Pope Wojtyla has not said or done anything about any of these things. Nevertheless, it is likely that von Balthasar, and later on Yves Congar, were named cardinals precisely because they had both raised such questions. Like von Balthasar, Congar had also discussed the use of papal titles, and both of them had taught that the Church is at once holy and a sinner (von Balthasar even published an essay titled *Casta Meretrix* [Chaste Prostitute]) and they had both insisted on the need for a continual reform of the Church (*Vraie et Fausse Reforme dans l'Eglise* [True and False Reform in the Church] by Congar, based on the ancient axiom, *Ecclesia semper reformanda est*, the Church is always in need of reform).[62] I personally believe that Pope John Paul wanted to reward them for having the courage to point out that the radical teaching of the Gospel was compatible with the needs of the institutional Church.

What Pope Wojtyla has said and done as regards the revision of the history of the papacy can be listed under three headings: general statements, symbolic gestures, and specific acknowledgments.

General Statements

The most important statement by Pope John Paul is the one contained in the Encyclical, *Ut Unum Sint* (1995), where he asks forgiveness from other Christians for the faults of the popes during the time of the division of the Churches:

> As I acknowledged on the important occasion of a visit to the World Council of Churches in Geneva on June 12, 1984, the Catholic Church's conviction that in the ministry of the Bishop of Rome she has preserved, in fidelity to the Apostolic Tradition and the faith of the

Fathers, the visible sign and guarantor of unity, constitutes a difficulty for most other Christians, whose
memory is marked by certain painful recollections. To
the extent that we are responsible for these, I join my
Predecessor Paul VI in asking forgiveness (*Ut Unum
Sint,* May 30, 1995; 88).

Two other general statements complete this confession of faults, and they pertain to the moral corruption
of persons at a high level of authority in the Church.
Both statements refer to the moral culpability of certain
popes in the history of the Church. The first was pronounced at Geneva in 1984, at a meeting of the World
Council of Churches:

Despite the moral afflictions which have marked the
life of its members and even of its leaders in the course
of history, it is convinced that in the ministry of the
Bishop of Rome it has preserved the visible pole and
guarantee of unity in full fidelity to the apostolic tradition and to the faith of the Fathers (Meeting of World
Council of Churches, Geneva, June 12, 1984).

The second statement was made four years later at
Nancy, France, during a homily at Mass, but not to an
ecumenical audience. Consequently, the confession of
fault is perhaps more forceful, although less precise in
its formulation:

The boat that is the Church is in the midst of the
world.... This boat has held up well and cleared a way in
the turbulence of history. Many events and evils have
troubled her peace from within and without: the first
persecutions at Jerusalem, then at Rome, starting with
Nero; ...then the theological quarrels that divided
Christians; the invasions that necessitated a new beginning of evangelization; the threat of the lessening, in-

deed the corruption of the moral and religious sense continuously requiring reform, as in the time of my predecessor Leo IX, former Bishop of Toul (Nancy, France, October 10, 1988).

Pope John Paul mentioned Pope Leo IX because he was an Alsatian, like the audience at Nancy. He is venerated as a saint and is considered by historians to be the greatest pope of German origin in the Middle Ages. As soon as he was elected, he instituted a drastic reform of morals at the papal court. But of the popes who had to struggle day and night against the corruption of the members of the Curia or of the popes who were themselves morally corrupt, Pope Wojtyla could have mentioned many others! This calm reference in the homily, which places moral corruption at the same level as ordinary evils in the hierarchy of the Church, is itself noteworthy. Both of the preceding statements are summarized in the following passage from the Encyclical, *Ut Unum Sint*:

> The Catholic Church thus affirms that during the two thousand years of her history she has been preserved in unity, with all the means with which God wishes to endow his Church, and this despite the often grave crises which have shaken her, the infidelity of some of her ministers, and the faults into which her members daily fall. The Catholic Church knows that, by virtue of the strength which comes to her from the Spirit, the weaknesses, mediocrity, sins and at times the betrayals of some of her children cannot destroy what God has bestowed on her as part of his plan of grace. Moreover, "the powers of death shall not prevail against her" (Mt 16:18). Even so, the Catholic Church does not forget that many among her members cause God's plan to be discernible only with difficulty (*Ut Unum Sint,* 11).

Symbolic Gestures

Under this heading we refer to the change of attitude or judgment concerning the history or practices of the papacy to which we have referred throughout the chapters of this book. Among the most significant ecumenical gestures we recall the papal visit to the synagogue in Rome, the numerous visits to churches of other communions, the veneration of the martyrs of Presov, the meeting with young people at Casablanca. Here, however, we shall pause a moment to consider the Pope's three visits to other Christian churches. They are a very special manifestation of humility in the attempt to change the anti-ecumenical spirit of the past.

The first, and perhaps the one of greatest symbolic value, is the visit to the Lutheran cathedral at Roskilde in Denmark in June, 1989. There the Pope took part in a prayer meeting, but he was not given an opportunity to speak. This was a shocking decision on the part of the Danish Church authorities and it caused a dispute even within the Danish Lutheran Church. Bertil Wiberg, the Lutheran bishop of Roskilde, explained why the Pope was not called upon to speak: "We did not want it to happen that on hearing him speak, some people would think that John Paul II was also our Pontiff. The Pope is welcome, but it must be remembered that it is we who received him and not he who received us."[63]

The second symbolic gesture occurred during that same visit to Scandinavia, in the cathedral of Uppsala, Sweden, in the presence of King Carl Gustaf and Queen Sylvia. The Lutheran bishop, Bertil Werstrom, embraced the Pope and reminded him that there, in that very church, in 1920, the ecumenical movement began under the leadership of the Lutheran Archbishop Nathan Söderblom. "On that day," said Bishop Werstrom,

"John the apostle was represented by the Orthodox prelate, Paul the apostle by the Lutheran archbishop. But the apostle Peter was absent. Today, however, Peter is here and he is called John Paul II."

The Pope then placed a floral wreath on the tomb of Archbishop Söderblom, against whom Pope Pius XI had taken a very negative attitude because of Söderblom's energetic support of the ecumenical movement. Pope Wojtyla stated that he had come there in a spirit of repentance and he asked for mutual forgiveness on both sides. We have already noted that on one occasion Karl Barth had asked the Catholic Church to acknowledge that others had been the progenitors of the ecumenical movement. Herein lies the symbolic significance of the gesture in which the Pope placed the floral wreath on the tomb of the Lutheran archbishop. In so doing, he was acknowledging Archbishop Söderblom as the founder of the ecumenical movement. Six years later, Pope John Paul referred to this explicitly in the Encyclical, *Ut Unum Sint*:

> The ecumenical movement really began within the churches and ecclesial communities of the Reform. At about the same time, in January, 1920, the Ecumenical Patriarchate expressed the hope that some kind of cooperation among the Christian communions could be organized. This fact shows that the weight of cultural background is not the decisive factor. What is essential is the question of faith. The prayer of Christ, our one Lord, Redeemer, and Master, speaks to everyone in the same way, both in the East and in the West. That prayer becomes an imperative to leave behind our divisions in order to seek and re-establish unity, as a result also of the bitter experiences of division itself (*Ut Unum Sint*, 65).

The third visit took place in June of 1991 in the Orthodox cathedral in Bialystok, Poland, near the border of Belarus. The symbolic value of that visit was the fact that the Pope went there to ask and grant forgiveness of his ecumenical hosts, who had constructed their church on the very site of the former Catholic cathedral, which had been destroyed by order of the Russian czar.

Specific Acknowledgments

Throughout this second part of the book we have mentioned specific historical cases in which the papacy must be held responsible. Now we shall add some others that we have not mentioned in particular or treated sufficiently: the intolerance of Catholics for non-Catholics when the popes had temporal power; the condemnation of the works of Antonio Rosmini; the question of religious freedom; the condemnation of Modernism at the beginning of the present century.

1. *The Lutherans in Rome When the Pope Had Temporal Power*. When Pope John Paul visited Christuskirche, the Lutheran church in Rome, in December, 1983, he recalled the "difficult history" of this Evangelical community. The phrase "difficult history" is a rather sober one, but it was very meaningful to his listeners. This particular Lutheran church was constructed in Rome after the end of the papal government and temporal power. Prior to that, the Lutherans in Rome had to gather for church services in the Prussian Embassy. Pope John Paul told them:

> We know the difficult history of this Evangelical Lutheran community in Rome: its painful beginning and the lights and shadows of its growth in the atmosphere of this city. It makes us ask ourselves with even

greater urgency: "In spite of all our human weakness and in spite of the lack of any historical foundation, can we trust in the grace of the Lord which has been manifested in these latter days through the words of the Holy Spirit that we have perceived during the Council?" (The Lutheran Church in Rome, December 11, 1983).

2. *Condemnation of Rosmini*. Pope John Paul II has authorized the opening of the cause for beatification of Antonio Rosmini, an author condemned by the Holy Office. Bishop Clemente Riva, a Rosminian, made the following comment in an interview with the magazine, *Trentagiorni*, in May, 1995:

> The condemnation of forty philosophical and theological propositions from the works of Rosmini, formulated by the Holy Office in 1887, is still a serious matter. But it is a question of a condemnation that is somewhat anomalous, since it was not accompanied by any theological explanation, as is usually the case. In 1973 Pope Paul VI named a commission, of which I was a member, in order to review the condemnation. After three years of discussion, each member of the commission made a personal evaluation which was sent to the Prefect of the Congregation for the Doctrine of the Faith, who at that time was Cardinal Seper. The conclusions written by the Croatian prelate were not favorable to Rosmini. The Congregation decided that "the suppression of the condemnation is neither well-grounded nor is it opportune." Five years ago the present Holy Father appointed a new commission, also made up this time of five prelates. Their conclusions, submitted a few years ago, have not been made public, but the Pope knows them. And, being aware of the conclusions of this commission, he has granted the *non obstat* for the process of beatification.[64]

3. *Religious Freedom and Modernism.* On June 26, 1990, the Congregation for the Doctrine of the Faith issued a document entitled *Instruction on the Ecclesial Vocation of the Theologian.* It was signed by Cardinal Ratzinger and promulgated with the approval of Pope John Paul II. The document states that perhaps it is the first time that the Congregation speaks with such clarity, asserting that the Magisterium, including that of the popes, can be mistaken when it makes pronouncements on "mixed matters," that is, "debated questions in which there are conjectural and contingent matters mixed in with firmly established principles." In some cases the Magisterium has made mistakes:

> The willingness to submit loyally to the teaching of the Magisterium on matters *per se* not irreformable must be the rule.... When it comes to the question of interventions in the prudential order, it could happen that some Magisterial documents might not be free from all deficiencies. Bishops and their advisors have not always taken into immediate consideration every aspect or the entire complexity of a question. But it would be contrary to the truth if, proceeding from some particular cases, one were to conclude that the Church's Magisterium can be habitually mistaken in its prudential judgments or that it does not enjoy divine assistance in the integral exercise of its mission (Congregation for the Doctrine of the Faith, June 26, 1990).

In presenting the document to the public, Cardinal Ratzinger cited two instances in which previous decisions have been overturned: "One can think of declarations by popes in the last century concerning religious freedom and also the statements against Modernism at the beginning of this century, especially the decisions of the Biblical Commission at that time."

TWENTY-ONE

The Blacks

If Pope John Paul II had not travelled as he did, perhaps he would not have asked for forgiveness. While this statement is true in general, it is especially true when we consider the treatment of Blacks. The Pope spoke of this matter on three special occasions: during the two visits to Africa (Cameroon [1985] and Senegal [1992]) and during his visit to Santo Domingo in 1992. On all three occasions he spoke with deep emotion and in a spirit of repentance. Later he spoke again of this question to a group of bishops from Brazil (1995), but his tone changed. In addition to asking forgiveness for what "not a few Christians" had done, he defended the popes for condemning the treatment of the Blacks and he asserted that the Church has never ceased to defend the rights of slaves. We have already seen this balance between injustices committed and the good that was done when we discussed the treatment of Indians in Chapter 10. But even then the most incisive words were uttered by the Pope during his travels around the world or as soon as he had returned home and the experiences were fresh in his mind; his words of praise or defense were usually spoken in public utterances in Rome.

We Ask Pardon of Our African Brothers and Sisters

The first request for forgiveness was spoken during the Pope's visit to Africa in 1985, a key event in the pontificate of Pope Wojtyla. It revealed his missionary spirit, permeated with a sense of his mission to the nations. On this particular journey he met with priests of the animistic religion in Togo, vehemently condemned apartheid, asked pardon for the treatment of Blacks, and made a beginning on a direct approach to Islam. In the same missionary spirit he spoke words of self-criticism, after reminding his listeners that Christianity defends freedom and the inalienable rights of the person:

> In the course of history, men belonging to Christian nations unfortunately have not always acted in this way and we ask forgiveness from our African brothers who have suffered so much; for example, because of the slave trade. Nevertheless, the Gospel continues to make its unequivocal appeal (Discourse to intellectuals, Cameroon, August 13, 1985).

From the Sanctuary of Suffering

Pope John Paul uttered his strongest words against the sinful treatment of Blacks in February, 1992, when he visited the island of Gorée (Senegal). He spoke about this twice; first when he visited the house of slaves, where he stated that the treatment of Blacks was "a tragedy of the civilization that claimed to be Christian." He then compared it to the treatment of persons in the extermination camps in Nazi Germany and said that the treatment in Africa was a "model" for the later injustices by persons who also "called themselves and claimed to be Christians." The text of his address is an outstanding Christian statement:

> I have come here to listen to the cry of the centuries and generations, the generations of Blacks, of slaves. Now, at the same time, I am thinking that Jesus Christ came, one might say, as a slave, a servant; but he brought light even into this situation of slavery. This light was called the presence of God, liberation in God...liberation in God, that is, the God who is Love.
>
> Here one thinks first and foremost about injustice: it is a tragedy of the civilization which claimed to be Christian. The great philosopher of antiquity, Socrates, said that those who find themselves in a situation of injustice are in a better condition than those who cause injustice.
>
> However, it is the other side of the reality of injustice which took place here. There is a human drama. This cry of the centuries, of generations, demands that we free ourselves ever more from this drama because the roots of this tragedy are in us, in human nature, in sin.
>
> I have come here to pay homage to all these victims, unknown victims; no one knows exactly how many there were; no one knows exactly who they were. Unfortunately, our civilization which called itself Christian, which claims to be Christian, returned to this situation of anonymous slaves in our century: we know what concentration camps were: here is a model for them. One cannot plumb the depths of the tragedy of our civilization, of our weakness, of sin. We must remain ever faithful to a different appeal, that of St. Paul who said: "Where sin abounded, grace abounded even more"; grace, that means love, abounded even more (Visit to the house of slaves, Gorée, Senegal, February 22, 1992).

Here is another text which is as beautiful as the one we just cited. It was addressed to the people on the island of Gorée on the same day and in it the Pope implored "heaven's forgiveness" for the sin of those persons "who did not live their faith." He prayed that "never again will people oppress their brothers and sisters":

> The visit to the "slave house" recalls to mind that enslavement of Black people which in 1462 Pius II, writing to a missionary bishop who was leaving for Guinea, described as the "enormous crime," the *magnum scelus.* Throughout a whole period of the history of the African continent, Black men, women and children were brought to this cramped space, uprooted from their land and separated from their loved ones to be sold as goods. They came from all different countries and, parting in chains for new lands, they retained as the last image of their native Africa Gorée's basalt rock cliffs. We could say that this island is fixed in the memory and heart of all the Black diaspora.
>
> These men, women and children were the victims of a disgraceful trade in which people who were baptized, but did not live their faith, took part. How can we forget the enormous suffering inflicted, the violation of the most basic human rights, on those people deported from the African continent? How can we forget the human lives destroyed by slavery?
>
> In all truth and humility this sin of man against man, this sin of man against God, must be confessed. How far the human family still has to go until its members learn to look at and respect one another as God's image, in order to love one another as sons and daughters of their common heavenly Father!
>
> From this African shrine of Black sorrow, we implore heaven's forgiveness. We pray that in the future Christ's disciples will be totally faithful to the observance of the commandment of fraternal love which the

Master left us. We pray that never again will people oppress their brothers and sisters, whoever they may be, but always seek to imitate the compassion of the Good Samaritan in the Gospel in going to help those who are in need. We pray that the scourge of slavery and all its effects may disappear forever. Do not recent tragic incidents on this continent too invite us to be watchful and continue this lengthy, laborious process of conversion of heart? We must equally oppose the new, often insidious forms of slavery, such as organized prostitution, which shamefully takes advantage of the poverty of the people of the Third World. (Meeting with the Catholic community, Gorée, Senegal, February 22, 1992).

The third confession of sin is contained in two distinct texts, one weak and another strong, both of which were read in October, 1992, on the solemn occasion commemorating the fifth centenary of the evangelization of Latin America:

Everyone is aware of the serious injustice committed against those Black peoples of the African continent who were violently torn from their land, their culture and their traditions, and shipped to America as slaves. During my recent apostolic visit to Senegal, I did not want to omit a visit to the island of Gorée, where this ignominious trade began. I wanted to show the Church's firm repudiation of it (Message to Afro-Americans, Santo Domingo, October 13, 1992).

On his return to Rome from his pilgrimage to Latin America, Pope John Paul told the people at a general audience that it had also been an act of atonement for the sin, injustice and violence that had accompanied the conquest and evangelization of Latin America. We have already referred to this text when we discussed the treatment of the Indians; but here we quote the passage that refers to the Blacks:

> We do not cease asking these people for "forgiveness."
> This request for pardon is primarily addressed to the
> first inhabitants of the new land, to the Indios, and
> then to those who were brought from Africa as slaves to
> do heavy labor (General audience, St. Peter's, October
> 21, 1992).

It should be noted that the Holy Father did not
speak about the treatment of Blacks only on the occasions that we have indicated. He also spoke about this
question on less solemn occasions, which shows that in a
relatively short time this had become a frequent topic in
the Pope's preaching. Thus, in the general audience on
March 4, 1992, he recalled his recent pilgrimage to Africa and the visit to the island of Gorée. He urged his
listeners to include that historical sin in their Lenten
penitential practices, thus acknowledging "in a spirit of
penance, all the crimes which in that long period were
perpetrated against the peoples of Africa by that shame-
ful trade."

Two years earlier, on a previous trip to Africa, the
Holy Father had said at Praia, Cape Verde, on January
26, 1990:

> Your land was formerly known as a strategic point for
> war and a place that shortened distances for trade. Un-
> fortunately, it was also known for the abominable trade
> in human persons during the time of slavery. It is like-
> wise possible that scars still remain in your culture be-
> cause of this. Today, with you here, I would like to stress
> two things which are a constant teaching of the
> ecclesial Magisterium. The first is: "No" to discrimina-
> tion of all types; never can there be enslavement of one
> person by another.

At other times the reference to the sinful treatment
of Blacks was not in the written text, but the Pope spoke

of it in a spontaneous manner, as if he felt that he had to say something to that particular audience. For example, he spoke as follows to the people on the island of Sao Tomé on June 6, 1992:

> On this island, a testimony to the tragic phenomenon of the slave trade, I cannot help but deplore—as I have already done at Gorée in Senegal—this cruel offense against the dignity of the African people. These sufferings of the past are for the Pope an occasion for greater love and solidarity for the people of Sao Tomé.

Previous Prohibitions Were Insufficient

After his impassioned remarks as a traveler and a guest of people who had been victims of raids and kidnappings for centuries, when the Pope was back in Rome he again returned to the question of slavery. This time he was addressing the bishops of Brazil during their *ad limina* visit. He reminded them of the division in the Brazilian episcopate when looking back on that tragic period:

> As regards slavery in Africa, I have already had an opportunity to implore heaven's forgiveness for the shameful slave trade between Africa and the newly discovered continent, in which many Christians took part to supply the work force.... The severe prohibitions of my venerable Predecessors, Pius II in 1462 and Urban VIII in 1623, were not enough in those deplorable times, nor were the invectives of Benedict XIV (cf. the papal Bull *Immensa Pastorum*), who even excommunicated those who sold and ill treated slaves, or who reduced Africans to slavery.
>
> Despite the society and culture of the age, the Church never ceased to defend the slaves against the unjust situation into which they had fallen victim, as attested for example by the Bahia Constitutions of 1707,

the first canonical legislation drafted in Brazilian territory, which sought to alleviate the terrible consequences of slavery as far as possible (canons 303 and
304) (Ad limina visit of Brazilian bishops, St. Peter's,
April 1, 1995).

Without judging the merit of the Pope's statements,
I shall simply quote the conclusion drawn by the Jesuit
historian, Giacomo Martina: "The Church, which under
Paul III and Urban VIII had effectively defended the
rights of the Indians, never raised its voice against the
slave trade until 1800. The documents that are usually
cited in this regard refer to the Indians; they do not
speak about the Blacks."[65]

Notes

[1] Hans Urs von Balthasar, *Who Is a Christian?,* tr. J. Cumming, New York: Newman Press, 1967, pp. 14-15, passim. The original German version was published in 1965.

[2] Cf. B. Mondin, *Dizionario Enciclopedico dei Papi,* Roma: Città Nuova, 1995, p. 312.

[3] *Tutte le Encicleche dei Sommi Pontefici,* Milano: Dall'Oglio, 1959, p. 190.

[4] Reported by Giacomo Martina, *La Chiesa nell'Età dell' Assolutismo, del Liberalismo, del Totalitarismo*, Brescia: Morcelliana, 1974, p. 419. New information regarding the failed attempts of the popes who did speak out against the evil of slavery has recently come to light and is documented by Joel Panzer in *The Popes and Slavery*, New York: Alba House, 1996.

[5] Cf. G.K.A. Bell, *Documents on Christian Unity,* London: Oxford University Press, 1924, p. 2.

[6] Cf. ibid., p. 7.

[7] Cf. W.A. Visser 'T Hooft (ed.), *The First Assembly of the World Council of Churches*, New York: Harper and Brothers, 1949, pp. 50-56.

[8] *The Second Assembly of the World Council of Churches,* 1954, London: SCM Press, 1955, pp. 87-89.

[9] In this book Rabbi Toaff states: "After promoting a reform of the liturgy for Good Friday by abolishing the phrase

'perfidious Jews,' he wanted, together with the Council, finally to do justice to the Jewish people whom he respected and loved. He demonstrated this repect and this love on a Saturday in the springtime when, passing along the Lungotevere, he saw the Jews coming out of the synagogue after prayer. He had the chauffeur stop the automobile and he blessed his Jewish brothers. They were naturally amazed at first, and then they surrounded him, applauding enthusiastically. It was the first time in history that a pope had ever blessed the Jews and it was perhaps the first gesture of reconciliation" (p. 219).

[10] Cf. Stjepan Schmidt, *Agostino Bea, il cardinale dell'unità*, Roma: Città Nuova, 1987, p. 351.

[11] Cf. *Council Daybook: Vatican II, Sessions 1 and 2,* Washington, DC: NCWC, 1966, p. 282.

[12] This letter is dated July 27, 1926.

[13] Quoted in *Avvenire d'Italia,* January 21, 1954.

[14] Recounted by Roger Schutz at the international gathering of youth at Notre Dame in Paris, December 29, 1978.

[15] *Council Daybook: Vatican II, Sessions 1 and 2,* p. 148.

[16] Ibid., p. 199.

[17] Cf. *Council Daybook: Vatican II, Session 4*, 1966, p. 286.

[18] Cf. Carlo Cremona, *Paolo VI,* Roma: Rusconi, 1992, p. 177.

[19] Karl Barth, *Ad Limina Apostolorum,* tr. K.R. Crim, Richmond: Knox Press, 1968, pp. 30-37, passim.

[20] Rocco Buttiglione, *"Il Mea Culpa della Chiesa: Non Sono Stupito"* in *La Voce,* April 16, 1994: "There are two factors that differentiate the history and culture of Poland from the history and culture of the rest of Europe. The first is the way Poland looked upon the Protestant Reformation. In other nations it led to the scandal of civil war and reciprocal funeral pyres; in Poland, on the other hand, Catholicism reacted to the reformation with another reform of an Erasmian type. In other words, there was no military repression of Protestants, but a Christianization of the masses that led to an absorption of the

Protestant secession. The second factor is that Poland has never witnessed an opposition between the nationalist cause and the Catholic cause, as we [the Italians] did in the *Risorgimento*. The Polish Garibaldis were Catholic, and some of them are in the process of beatification. Here too, there was no contrast between the cause of God and the cause of man, which later brought about the laicist confrontation. While the rest of Europe followed the principle, *cuius regio eius religio* (every subject must follow the religion of his king), the King of Poland asked: 'Am I perhaps the master of the conscience of my subjects?'"

[21] Karol Wojtyla, *Collected Poems,* tr. by Jerzy Peterkiewicz, New York: Random House, 1982, p. 139.

[22] Copernicus's work, *De Revolutionibus Orbium Coelestium* was published in 1543 and it was not placed on the *Index* until 1616, after the first condemnation of Galileo. In commemorating Copernicus on October 18, 1993, 450 years after his death, Pope John Paul contrasted the difference in attitude between the Polish and the Italian astronomers: the first had the prudence to present his theory as a hypothesis; the other put it forward as a scientific certainty. Pope Wojtyla praised "the prudence and courage with which Copernicus tried to harmonize freedom of scientific investigation with loyalty to the Church."

[23] Cf. *Karol Wojtyla negli Scritti. Bibliografia*, Città del Vaticano: Libreria Editrice Vaticana, 1980, p. 245, n. 1207.

[24] Cf. *Council Daybook: Vatican II, Session 3,* Washington, DC: NCWC, 1965, p. 36.

[25] For example, this was the objection voiced by Franz Schmidberger, the successor of Lefebvre as head of the Fraternity of Econe.

[26] From an interview published by *La Repubblica*, January 19, 1996.

[27] Reported in *Corriere della Sera,* June 15, 1994.

[28] Cf. Giacomo Biffi, *Christus Hodie,* Bologna: EDB, 1995, pp. 23-24.

[29] A position similar to that of Cardinal Biffi was taken by Bishop Maggiolini of Como, Italy. One of the strongest opponents of the Pope's project is Antonio Socci, former director of the magazine *Trentagiorni (30 Days)*. The journalist Renato Farina came to the defense of the Pope's proposal. Outside of Italy, another notable critic is the Church historian, Walter Brandmüller, professor at the University of Augsburg, Germany.

[30] In the spring and early summer of 1994, Pope John Paul II performed a series of actions that contributed greatly to the ecumenical progress desired by the Second Vatican Council: the promulgation of the Encyclical *Ut Unum Sint* (May 30); asking and offering pardon for the wars of religion (May 21); veneration of the Protestant Slovak martyrs (July 2); meeting with the Patriarch of Constantinople (June 27-30). Konrad Reiser, director general of the ecumenical council at Geneva, stated that the gestures of the Pope could "inspire us to close the books on our controversies of the past."

[31] Between June and September of 1994, the Pope referred at least five times to this topic.

[32] This is by far the largest commission. It has twenty-six members: the Jesuits P.M. de Franca Miranda, Michael McDermott, Albert Canhoye; the Salesians Sebastian Kerotemprel, Raffaele Farina, Angelo Amato; the Dominicans Guy Bedouelle, Simon Tugwell; the Capuchins Yannis Spiteris, William Henn; the Sulpician John Dorè; the Redemptorist Réal Tremblay; the diocesan priests Franco Topic, Lukasz Kamykowski, Piero Coda, Luis Illanes, John Egbulefu, Salvador Pié-Ninot, Henrique Galvao de Noronha, Hermann Josef Pottmeyer, Jean Corbon; three religious without identification: Julien Efoè Penoukou, Jean Stern, Jean-Miguel Garrigues; and the lay persons Gösta Hallonsten and Maria Ko (as of February, 1996).

[33] Cf. Giacomo Martina, *La Chiesa nell'Età dell'Assolutismo, del Liberalismo, del Totalitarismo*, Brescia: Morcelliana, 1974, p. 291.

[34] Quoted in *Avvenire*, February 14, 1995, p. 19.

[35] This document was published in *Il Regno,* November, 1996, pp. 367-73.

[36] The text of the Pope's memorandum to the cardinals was never published officially by the Vatican. It was publicized by the agency ADN-Kronos and later the entire text was published by the agency ADISTA, on May 28, 1994. For an up-to-date study of one of the major ecumenical questions facing the Church, see *Apostolic Succession in an Ecumenical Context* by Thomas M. Kocik, New York: Alba House, 1996.

[37] Hans Küng, *Reforming the Church Today*, tr. Peter Heinegg et al., New York: Crossroad, 1990, p. 102.

[38] Discourse at the General Chapter of the Congregation of Our Lady of Sion, January 15, 1964.

[39] Quoted in *Corriere della Sera,* December 3, 1985.

[40] Cf. *Corriere della Sera*, December 6, 1990.

[41] Quoted in *Corriere della Sera,* October 5, 1983.

[42] Cf. A. Segre, *Il Popolo di Israele e la Chiesa*, Roma: Centro pro Unione, 1982; I. Sestieri and G. Cereti, *Le Chiese Cristiane e l'Ebraismo,* Casale Monferrato: Marietti, 1983.

[43] Georges Cottier, OP, *"La Chiesa Davanti alla Conversione,"* in AA.VV., *Tertio Millennio Adveniente: Testo e Commento Teologico-Pastorale*, Cinisello Balsamo: San Paolo, 1996, p. 164.

[44] Cf. Georges Cottier, OP, art. cit., p. 166.

[45] Cf. *Council Daybook: Vatican II, Session 4,* Washington: NCWC, 1966, p. 36.

[46] Reported in *Segnosette*, June 4, 1995.

[47] Giovanni Franzoni, *Lasciate Riposare la Terra,* Roma: Edizioni dell'Università Popolare, 1996, p. 94.

[48] Georges Cottier, OP, *"La Chiesa Davanti alla Conversione,"* op. cit., p. 238.

[49] Published in *Avvenire*, February 14, 1995, p. 19. For an up-to-date study of Muslim-Christian relations in the Church, see *Muslims and Christians: Enemies or Brothers?* by Jean-René Milot, New York: Alba House, 1997.

[50] Pope John Paul stated that an excommunication ends with death in an address to the bishops of Denmark in Copenhagen. It was reported in *L'Osservatore Romano,* July 7, 1989.

[51] Published in *Corriere della Sera,* December 12, 1983, p. 1.

[52] Reported by Carlo Fiore in *La Sfida dell'Ecumenismo,* Torino: Elle Di Ci, 1995, p. 36.

[53] Published in *Corriere della Sera,* April 11, 1985, p. 1.

[54] Cf. Bartolomeo Sorge, S.J., *La Chiesa e la Mafia,* published in *Civiltà Cattolica,* III, 1995, pp. 496-504.

[55] Reported in *Corriere della Sera,* September 15, 1982.

[56] Cf. *L'Osservatore Romano,* September 16, 1987.

[57] Published in *Missione Oggi,* May, 1995, p. 7.

[58] Reported in *Corriere della Sera,* June 22, 1994, p. 2.

[59] See *Trentagiorni,* October, 1995, p. 19.

[60] *Service d'Information,* Pontifical Council for the Promotion of Christian Unity, n. 83, 1993.

[61] Hans Urs von Balthasar made his suggestion regarding the transfer of the pope to the gates of Rome in *Punti Fermi,* Milano: Rusconi, 1972, p. 326; for more about his opinion regarding the use of ecclesiastical titles, cf. *Sponsa Verbi,* Brescia: Morcelliana, 1969, p. 385; on infallibility, cf. *Avvenire,* February, 1980.

[62] Yves Congar published an article on the titles of the pope in *Concilium,* December, 1975. Among theologians who were named cardinals by Pope John Paul II, we could also add the name of Henri de Lubac who also felt that a re-examination of the history of the Church was in order. See his book, *Meditazione sulla Chiesa,* Milano, Jaca, 1979, originally published in French in 1953.

[63] Cf. D. Del Rio, *Wojtyla. Un Pontificato Itinerante,* Bologna: EDB, 1994, p. 625.

[64] Cf. *Trentagiorni,* May, 1995, pp. 54-55. Previously, Pope John Paul I had confided to Father Germano Pattaro his intention to rehabilitate Rosmini. He described Rosmini as "a priest who loved the Church, who suffered for the Church. He was a man of vast culture, of an integrated Christian faith; a master of philosophical and moral wisdom who saw clearly in the structure of the Church the evangelical and pastoral procrasti-

nation and non-implementation of the Gospel message. I want to find an opportunity to speak about Rosmini and his work, which I have reread very carefully.... We shall do this calmly, but we shall do it." For more details, cf. Camillo Bassotto, *Il Mio Cuore é Ancora a Venezia,* p. 131.

[65] Cf. Giacomo Martina, *La Chiesa nell'Età dell'Assolutismo, del Liberalismo, del Totalitarismo,* p. 415. For a documentation of the opposing point of view regarding the failed attempts of the popes who *did* speak out against the evil of slavery, see Joel Panzer, *The Popes and Slavery,* New York: Alba House, 1996.

Bibliography

Encyclicals, Boston:
Pauline Books & Media, 1975-1996:

On Evangelization in the Modern World (Evangelii Nuntiandi), Paul VI, Dec. 8, 1975.

Consecrated Life (Vita Consecrata), John Paul II, Mar. 25, 1996.

Letter of Pope John Paul II to Women, John Paul II, Feb. 2, 1994.

The Light of the East (Orientale Lumen), John Paul II, May 2, 1995.

On Commitment to Ecumenism (Ut Unum Sint), John Paul II, May 25, 1995.

On Social Concern (Solicitudo Rei Socialis), John Paul II, Dec. 30, 1987.

On the Dignity and Vocation of Women (Mulieris Dignitatem), John Paul II, Aug. 15, 1988.

Tertio Millennio Adveniente, John Paul II, Nov. 10, 1994.

On Reconciliation and Penance in the Mission of the Church Today (Reconciliatio et Paenitentia), Dec. 2, 1984.

Vatican II: The Conciliar and Post-Conciliar Documents, revised edition, Austin Flannery, OP, ed., Boston: St. Paul Editions, 1988.

**Also for individual documents cited in this book,
Boston: Pauline Books & Media:**

Declaration on the Relation of the Church to Non-Christian Religions (Nostra Aetate), Oct. 28, 1965.

Decree on Ecumenism (Unitatis Redintegratio), Nov. 21, 1964.

Decree on the Catholic Churches of the Eastern Rite (Orientalium Ecclesiarum), Nov. 21, 1964.

Decree on the Mission Activity of the Church (Ad Gentes), Dec. 7, 1965.

Dogmatic Constitution on the Church (Lumen Gentium), Nov. 21, 1964.

Pastoral Constitution on the Church in the Modern World (Gaudium et Spes), Dec. 7, 1965.

On CD Rom:

Church Documents: Third Edition, Boston: Pauline Books & Media, 1996.

Other Works:

Barth, Karl. *Ad Limina Apostolorum,* tr. K.R. Crim, Richmond: Knox Press, 1968.

Bell, G.K.A. *Documents on Christian Unity*, London: Oxford University Press, 1924.

Council Daybook: Vatican II, Sessions 1 and 2, Washington, DC: NCWC, 1966.

Kocik, Thomas M. *Apostolic Succession in an Ecumenical Context,* New York: Alba House, 1996.

Küng, Hans. *Reforming the Church Today,* tr. Peter Heinegg et al., New York: Crossroad, 1990.

Milot, Jean-René. *Muslims and Christians: Enemies or Brothers?,* New York: Alba House, 1997.

Neuner, J., S.J. and Dupuis, J., S.J., eds. *The Christian Faith in the Doctrinal Documents of the Catholic Church,* 6th Revised and Enlarged Edition, New York: Alba House, 1996.

Panzer, Joel. *The Popes and Slavery,* New York: Alba House, 1996.

Saward, John. *Christ Is the Answer: The Christ-Centered Teaching of Pope John Paul II,* New York: Alba House, 1995.

The Second Assembly of the World Council of Churches, 1954, London: SCM Press, 1955.

Visser 'T Hooft, W. A., (ed.). *The First Assembly of the World Council of Churches,* New York: Harper and Brothers, 1949.

von Balthasar, Hans Urs. *Who is a Christian?,* tr. J. Cumming, New York: Newman Press, 1967.

Wojtyla, Karol. *Collected Poems,* tr. by Jerzy Peterkiewicz, New York: Random House, 1982.